HARDWARE INTERFACES AND ITS APPLICATION

HARDWARE INTERFACES AND ITS APPLICATION

Manju C. Nair
Associate Professor,
Dept of CSE, Sathyabama Institute
of Science and Technology

R. Lalitha
Associate Professor,
Dept of CSE, Sathyabama Institute
of Science and Technology

Dharani V.
Associate Professor,
Dept of CSE, Sathyabama Institute
of Science and Technology

KHANNA BOOK PUBLISHING CO. (P) Ltd.
4C/4344, Ansari Road, Darya Ganj,
New Delhi, India

Sathyabama Institute of Science and Technology
Jeppiaar Nagar, Rajiv Gandhi Salai,
Chennai, Tamilnadu, India

Dear Readers,

To prevent the piracy, this book is secured with HIGH SECURITY HOLOGRAM on the front title cover. In case you don't find the hologram on the front cover title, please write us to at contact@khannabooks.com or whatsapp us at +91-99109 09320 and avail special gift voucher for yourself.

Specimen of Hologram on front Cover title:

Moreover, there is a SPECIAL DISCOUNT COUPON for you with EVERY HOLOGRAM.

How to avail this SPECIAL DISCOUNT:

Step 1: Scratch the hologram
Step 2: Under the scratch area, your "coupon code" is available
Step 3: Logon to www.khannabooks.com
Step 4: Use your "coupon code" in the shopping cart and get your copy at a special discount
Step 5: Enjoy your reading!

Thanks,
Khanna Publishing House

ISBN: 978-93-55386-43-4

HARDWARE INTERFACES AND ITS APPLICATION

by **Manju C. Nair, R. Lalitha, Dharani V.**

First Edition: 2026

To view complete list of books, please scan the QR Code:

Published by:
Khanna Book Publishing Co. (P) Ltd.
CIN: U22110DL1998PTC095547

Visit us at: www.khannabooks.com
Write us at: contact@khannabooks.com

Printed in Bharat.

Preface

The rapid advancement of computing technology has led to an increased reliance on efficient and well-integrated hardware systems. From personal computers and enterprise servers to cloud computing and IoT devices, hardware interfaces play a critical role in determining the performance, reliability, and functionality of modern computing systems. Recognizing the need for a comprehensive and structured resource on this subject, we have authored Hardware Interfaces and Its Application to serve as a guide for students, professionals, and technology enthusiasts.

This book is designed to provide a thorough understanding of the fundamental and advanced concepts related to computer hardware. Beginning with the evolution of personal computers and memory architectures, it delves into motherboard designs, power supplies, storage technologies, I/O peripherals, bus architectures, and network components. Each chapter is structured to progressively build knowledge, enabling readers to grasp both theoretical principles and real-world applications.

The primary objective of this book is to bridge the gap between foundational learning and industry requirements. As technology continues to evolve, learners must stay updated with emerging trends and developments. Therefore, we have incorporated discussions on modern processor architectures, high-speed storage interfaces, advanced networking protocols, and future directions in hardware innovation.

The content has been carefully curated to cater to different levels of expertise. Whether you are a beginner looking for a solid foundation in computer hardware or an experienced professional seeking to deepen your knowledge, this book offers insights that will be useful in academic, research, and industrial settings.

We extend our sincere gratitude to all those who have supported and contributed to the completion of this work. We hope that Hardware Interfaces and Its Application will serve as a valuable reference, guiding readers towards a deeper appreciation of the complexities and possibilities of computer hardware.

With best wishes,
Manju C Nair, R Lalitha, Dharani V

Contents

INTRODUCTION TO PC AND MEMORY

1

UNIT

RATIONALE

Computers have become an essential part of daily life, impacting industries, businesses, research, and education. Understanding the evolution of personal computers, types of memory, and their role in computing is fundamental for students entering the field of information technology. This unit provides foundational knowledge on computer hardware components, storage devices, and memory technologies, enabling learners to make informed decisions about system configurations and performance optimization.

OUTCOMES

After completing this unit, students will be able to:

1. Explain the evolution of personal computers and their impact on technology.
2. Identify different types of memory architectures and their role in computing.
3. Describe data storage devices and their performance characteristics.
4. Apply memory optimization techniques for efficient system performance.
5. Discuss real-world applications and industrial uses of various memory technologies.

1.1 EVOLUTION OF PERSONAL COMPUTERS

History and Generations of Computers

Early Mechanical Computers

The evolution of personal computers began with mechanical devices designed for calculations. Some of the earliest computing devices include:

- **Abacus (Circa 2400 B(c):** Used for basic arithmetic operations.
- **Pascaline (1642):** Designed by Blaise Pascal, one of the first mechanical calculators.
- **Difference Engine (1822):** Conceptualized by Charles Babbage, known as the 'Father of the Computer'.
- **Analytical Engine (1837):** An advanced mechanical computer proposed by Babbage with a punch-card programming concept.

First Generation (1940-1956) - Vacuum Tube Computers

- Vacuum tubes are used for circuitry, and magnetic drums are used for memory.
- Large in size and consumed high power.
- Examples are ENIAC (Electronic Numerical Integrator and Computer) and UNIVAC-I (Universal Automatic Computer).

Second Generation (1956-1963) - Transistor-Based Computers

- Replaced vacuum tubes with transistors, making computers smaller and more efficient.
- Used magnetic core memory and early forms of assembly language.
- Example: IBM 1401, PDP-1.

Third Generation (1964-1971) - Integrated Circuits (ICs)

- The introduction of ICs led to further miniaturization and improved performance.
- Introduction of keyboards and monitors as input/output devices.
- Example: IBM System/360, DEC PDP-8.

Fourth Generation (1971-Present) - Microprocessors

- The introduction of microprocessors (single-chip CPUs) revolutionized computing.
- Personal computers (PCs) became widely available.
- Examples are Apple I, IBM PC, Intel 8086, and AMD processors.

Fifth Generation (Present and Beyon(d) - AI and Quantum Computing

- Focuses on artificial intelligence (AI) and machine learning.
- Quantum computing and nanotechnology are emerging fields.
- Examples are IBM Watson and Google Quantum Computer.

Impact of Generational Advancements

Each generation of computers has contributed to the following:

- **Enhanced processing speed** with reduced physical size.
- **Increased accessibility** and affordability for businesses and individuals.
- **Development of modern computing applications** such as cloud computing, AI, and the Internet of Things (IoT).

Interesting Facts

- **Ancient Beginnings:** The abacus, dating back to 2400 BC, is one of the earliest known computing devices used for arithmetic calculations.
- **Mechanical Pioneers:** Devices like Pascal's Pascaline (1642) and Babbage's Difference Engine (1822) laid the groundwork for modern computers.
- **Revolutionary Generations:** The evolution from vacuum tube computers in the first generation to AI and quantum computing in the fifth generation illustrates dramatic leaps in speed, miniaturization, and capability.
- **Personal Computing Boom:** The introduction of microprocessors in the fourth generation sparked the personal computer revolution, making computing accessible to millions worldwide.
- **Future Frontiers:** The fifth generation, focusing on AI and quantum computing, is set to transform not only personal computing but also entire industries through enhanced machine learning and complex problem-solving.

Video Resources

- **Overview Videos:** Search for "History of Personal Computers" or "Evolution of Computers: From Abacus to AI" on YouTube for animated timelines and expert narrations.
- **Documentaries:** Look up "The Computer Revolution" and "The Rise of the Personal Computer" to see historical footage and interviews with pioneers like Babbage and early computer engineers.
- **Technical Deep Dives:** Channels like Computerphile and Techquickie provide in-depth explanations of how technologies like microprocessors and integrated circuits changed computing.

Use of ICT

- **Digital Transformation:** The evolution of personal computers illustrates the power of ICT in transforming society—from enabling early mechanical calculations to powering modern cloud computing and AI.
- **Connectivity and Collaboration:** Advances in computing have revolutionized communication, enabling global networks, online collaboration, and real-time data sharing.
- **Education and Research:** Personal computers have democratized access to information, transforming how education and research are conducted through online resources, simulations, and virtual labs.

Applications (Real Life/Industrial)

- **Everyday Use:** Today's personal computers are indispensable for tasks ranging from word processing and gaming to complex data analysis and digital content creation.
- **Business and Industry:** Modern PCs support industries with software for design, accounting, engineering, and communication, driving productivity and innovation.
- **Emerging Technologies:** The evolution of PCs has enabled the development of cloud computing, the Internet of Things (IoT), and AI-driven applications, influencing sectors like healthcare, finance, and education.

Case Study (Environmental/Sustainability/Social/Ethical Issues)

Context

A well-known urban school district implemented a computer literacy program to bridge the digital divide, but rapidly outdated hardware led to mounting electronic waste and energy inefficiencies.

Scenario

- **Challenge** The district's older PCs, based on outdated technologies, consumed high amounts of power and produced significant e-waste, straining both budgets and the local environment.

- **Solution:**
  - **Modernization:** The district upgraded to energy-efficient, modern PCs with microprocessor-based architectures and solid-state drives, which use less power and last longer.
  - **Recycling Program:** Partnered with local e-waste recycling centres to safely dispose of old hardware.
  - **Sustainability Education:** Integrated lessons on digital sustainability and responsible recycling into the curriculum.
- **Impact**
  - **Cost Savings:** Reduced energy costs and maintenance expenses.
  - **Environmental Benefit:** Lowered carbon footprint and minimized e-waste through efficient recycling.
  - **Social Impact:** Improved digital literacy and providing equitable access to modern technology, helping close the digital divide.

Discussion Points

- How do modern, energy-efficient PCs contribute to environmental sustainability in educational institutions?
- What ethical responsibilities do organizations have to upgrade technology while minimizing e-waste?
- How can digital literacy programs incorporate lessons on sustainable technology practices?

Create Inquisitiveness and Curiosity

- **Future Vision:** How might the next generation of personal computers—powered by quantum and AI technologies—transform everyday life?
- **Design Challenge:** Imagine designing a low-power, high-performance personal computer for remote areas with limited infrastructure. What technologies and design principles could be incorporated?
- **Debate Prompt:** Should governments invest more in recycling and sustainability initiatives for digital devices or focus on subsidizing technology upgrades to bridge the digital divide?
- **Innovation Brainstorm:** Can we conceptualize a hybrid computing device that combines the portability of mobile devices with the processing power of desktop PCs while being environmentally sustainable?

Solved Problems (With Increasing Difficulty Level)

Problem 1 (Basic)

Question

What was the significance of the Analytical Engine proposed by Charles Babbage?

Solution

The Analytical Engine, proposed by Babbage in 1837, was significant because it introduced the concept of programmable computing using punch cards, laying the groundwork for modern computers.

Problem 2 (Intermediate)

Question

Compare the advantages of transistor-based computers (second generation) to vacuum tube computers (first generation).

Solution

Transistor-based computers were smaller, more energy-efficient, and more reliable than vacuum tube computers. They reduced power consumption, generated less heat, and improved overall system performance, enabling broader use in various applications.

Problem 3 (Advanced)

Question

Explain how the introduction of microprocessors in the fourth generation revolutionized personal computing.

Solution

The introduction of microprocessors integrated the CPU onto a single chip, drastically reducing the size, cost, and power consumption of computers. This innovation made personal computers accessible to a broader audience, spurring the development of user-friendly operating systems, software applications, and, ultimately, the digital revolution that transformed business, education, and daily life.

Problem 4 (Challenging)

Question

Discuss how the evolution from early mechanical computers to modern AI-powered systems has impacted society, considering both technological advancements and social implications.

Solution

The evolution of computers has led to exponential improvements in processing power, miniaturization, and accessibility, transforming industries and daily life. Early mechanical devices enabled basic calculations, while vacuum tubes and transistors paved the way for electronic computing. The advent of microprocessors democratized access to technology, fostering innovation in personal computing. Today, AI-powered systems drive automation, data analytics, and decision-making across sectors. However, this evolution also brings challenges, such as the digital divide, e-waste management, and ethical concerns around data privacy and surveillance. Balancing technological progress with social responsibility remains a critical ongoing challenge.

1.2 OVERVIEW OF SYSTEMS AND COMPONENTS

A computer system consists of several fundamental components that work together to perform various computational tasks. Understanding these components is essential to grasp how computers function efficiently. The primary elements include the Central Processing Unit (CPU), Memory, Storage, Input/Output Devices, Motherboard, and Power

Supply Unit. Each component plays a crucial role in the system's overall performance and functionality.

Basic Structure of a Computer System

The structure of a computer system follows the Von Neumann architecture, which consists of a CPU, memory unit, and input/output devices connected through a system bus. The CPU acts as the brain of the computer, processing instructions and executing tasks. Memory units provide temporary and permanent storage for data, while input and output devices facilitate interaction between the user and the machine. The system bus enables communication among all these components. **Figure 1.1** below is a simplified diagram representing the Von Neumann architecture:

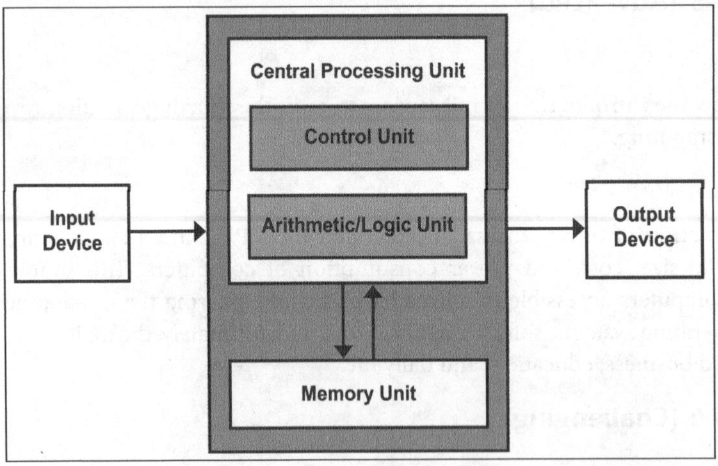

Figure 1.1: *Von Neumann Architecture*

Key Components of a Computer System

The Central Processing Unit (CPU) is responsible for executing instructions from programs. It comprises the Arithmetic Logic Unit (ALU) for performing mathematical operations and logical decisions, the Control Unit (CU) for directing operations within the processor, and registers for temporary data storage. Modern processors also feature multiple cores, enhancing multitasking capabilities and performance efficiency. **Table 1.1** presents a comparison of different CPU architectures, highlighting the key differences between single-core and multi-core processors. Multi-core processors offer superior processing power, efficiency, and multitasking capabilities while consuming less power per core compared to single-core processors.

Table 1.1: *Comparison of Different CPU Architectures*

Feature	Single-Core Processor	Multi-Core Processor
Processing Power	Limited	High
Efficiency	Low	High
Multitasking	Poor	Excellent
Power Consumption	More	Less per Core

Memory plays a crucial role in storing and retrieving data for processing. The two primary types of memory are Random Access Memory (RAM) and Read-Only Memory (ROM). RAM is a volatile memory that temporarily holds active programs and data, ensuring quick access by the processor. In contrast, ROM is non-volatile and contains essential firmware, including the computer's startup instructions. Figure 1.2 below is a a diagram showing the difference between RAM and ROM:

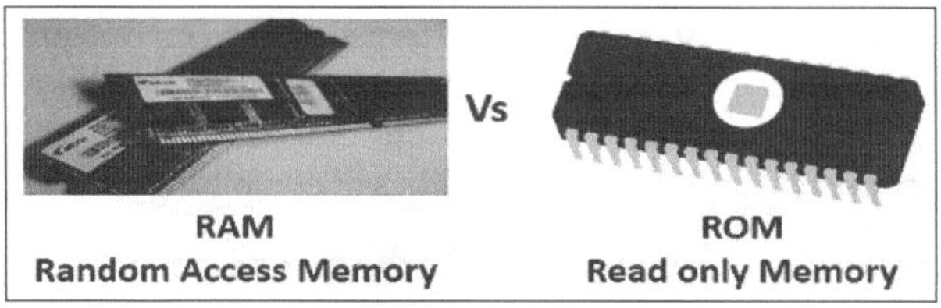

Figure 1.2: *RAM vs. ROM*

Storage devices provide long-term data retention, enabling users to save files, applications, and operating system data. The two main types of storage are Hard Disk Drives (HDDs) and Solid-State Drives (SSDs). HDDs utilize magnetic disks for data storage, offering larger capacities at an economical price. SSDs, on the other hand, employ flash memory, resulting in significantly faster read/write speeds and improved reliability.

Table 1.2 compares HDD and SSD storage technologies, outlining their key differences in performance, durability, cost, and power consumption. SSDs offer faster speeds, lower power consumption, and more excellent durability, whereas HDDs remain a cost-effective option with higher storage capacity per dollar.

Table 1.2: *Comparison of HDD and SSD*

Feature	HDD	SSD
Speed	Slower	Faster
Durability	Mechanical Parts	No Moving Parts
Price	Cheaper	Expensive
Power Consumption	Higher	Lower

Interaction Between Hardware and Software

Hardware and software work in unison to deliver computing functions. The Operating System (OS) serves as an intermediary between hardware components and software applications, managing resources such as memory allocation, processing tasks, and peripheral control. When a user runs an application, the OS coordinates the interaction between the software and the computer's hardware.

For example, when a word processing application is launched, the OS loads it into RAM, assigns CPU resources for execution, and facilitates input/output operations through peripherals like the keyboard and monitor. Device drivers play a crucial role in enabling communication between the OS and hardware devices, ensuring seamless functionality.

Role of the Operating System in Hardware Management

The OS performs several key functions in managing hardware resources effectively. Process management involves allocating CPU time to running programs, ensuring efficient multitasking. Memory management optimizes RAM usage by allocating and deallocating memory space as needed.

Device management controls input and output operations, facilitating communication between hardware peripherals and the system. Additionally, file system management ensures organized data storage and retrieval. Security management safeguards system resources from unauthorized access, malware, and other threats.

Computers have evolved significantly in terms of system design and architecture, improving their speed, efficiency, and user-friendliness. Modern systems integrate advanced features such as cloud computing, virtualization, and artificial intelligence, enhancing overall productivity and expanding the possibilities of computing applications.

Role of the Operating System in Hardware Management

The OS performs several key functions in managing hardware resources effectively. Process management involves allocating CPU time to running programs, ensuring efficient multitasking. Memory management optimizes RAM usage by allocating and deallocating memory space as needed.

Device management controls input and output operations, facilitating communication between hardware peripherals and the system. Additionally, file system management ensures organized data storage and retrieval. Security management safeguards system resources from unauthorized access, malware, and other threats.

Computers have evolved significantly in terms of system design and architecture, improving their speed, efficiency, and user-friendliness. Modern systems integrate advanced features such as cloud computing, virtualization, and artificial intelligence, enhancing overall productivity and expanding the possibilities of computing applications.

Interesting Facts

- **Von Neumann Architecture:** Modern computer systems are built on the Von Neumann architecture, where a single system bus connects the CPU, memory, and input/output devices, enabling efficient communication.
- **CPU as the Brain:** The Central Processing Unit (CPU) is often called the "brain" of the computer, comprising components like the Arithmetic Logic Unit (ALU) and Control Unit (CU), with modern CPUs featuring multiple cores to enhance multitasking.
- **Memory Duality:** RAM (volatile memory) provides fast, temporary storage for active processes, while ROM (non-volatile) retains crucial firmware even without power.
- **Storage Evolution:** HDDs use magnetic disks to offer economical high-capacity storage, whereas SSDs use flash memory for faster, more reliable data access.
- **Hardware-Software Synergy:** The operating system (OS) acts as the intermediary between hardware and software, ensuring that every component, from the keyboard to the hard drive, works together seamlessly.

Video Resources

- **Overview Videos:** Search for "Overview of Computer Systems" or "Von Neumann Architecture Explained" on YouTube to find animated guides and historical overviews.

- **Tutorials:** Look up "How CPUs Work" and "Understanding RAM vs. ROM" for detailed technical breakdowns and demonstrations.
- **Expert Discussions:** Channels like Computer phile and Tech quickie offer engaging explanations on topics like multi-core processors, storage evolution, and OS resource management.

Use of ICT

- **Digital Transformation:** ICT has transformed the way we interact with technology by integrating sophisticated hardware with intuitive software, enabling everything from cloud computing to real-time data analytics.
- **Resource Management:** ICT tools (like system monitors and diagnostic software) help manage memory, CPU usage, and storage, ensuring optimal performance and quick troubleshooting.
- **Virtualization & Cloud Services:** Modern ICT leverages virtualization to run multiple operating systems on a single physical machine, enhancing resource utilization and flexibility in enterprise environments.

Applications (Real Life/Industrial)

- **Personal Computing:** Everyday tasks such as web browsing, document editing, and gaming rely on the efficient interplay of CPU, memory, and storage.
- **Business & Enterprise:** Advanced computer systems power financial modelling, design software, and data analytics, driving productivity across industries.
- **Education & Research:** Schools and research institutions use modern computing systems for simulations, data analysis, and online learning, fostering innovation and knowledge sharing.
- **Industrial Automation:** Embedded systems in manufacturing use streamlined computer components to control machinery, monitor processes, and improve safety and efficiency.

Case Study (Environmental/Sustainability/Social/Ethical Issues)

Context

A large urban school district implemented a technology upgrade program to provide students with modern personal computers. However, the rapid obsolescence of hardware posed significant environmental challenges due to increasing electronic waste.

Scenario

- **Challenge:** The district's older systems were based on outdated architectures with high energy consumption and short lifespans, leading to increased electronic waste and higher operational costs.
- **Solution:**
    - **System Modernization:** The district upgraded to energy-efficient PCs featuring multi-core CPUs, SSD storage, and improved memory management based on modern Von Neumann architecture.

  - **E-Waste Recycling:** A comprehensive recycling program was established to dispose of obsolete equipment responsibly.
  - **Sustainability Education:** The curriculum was updated to include lessons on digital sustainability, teaching students the importance of recycling and energy-efficient technology.
- **Impact:**
  - **Cost Savings:** Newer systems reduced energy usage and maintenance costs.
  - **Environmental Benefits:** The recycling program and energy-efficient hardware contributed to a lower carbon footprint.
  - **Social Impact:** Improved access to modern technology helped bridge the digital divide and provided students with skills for the future.

Discussion Points

- How do modern computer components contribute to energy efficiency and lower environmental impact?
- What are the ethical responsibilities of institutions in managing electronic waste while upgrading technology?
- How can educational programs incorporate lessons on sustainable technology use?

Create Inquisitiveness and Curiosity

- **Future Vision:** How might emerging processor technologies (like quantum computing or neuromorphic chips) further revolutionize the fundamental architecture of computer systems?
- **Design Challenge:** Imagine designing a computer system that maximizes both performance and sustainability. What hardware and architectural choices could be made?
- **Debate Prompt:** Should the focus of computer system evolution be on maximizing speed and capacity or on improving energy efficiency and sustainability? What are the trade-offs?
- **Innovation Brainstorm:** Can we propose a new model of computer architecture that integrates advanced memory management and low-power components to achieve both high performance and eco-friendliness?

Solved Problems (With Increasing Difficulty Level)

Problem 1 (Basic)

Question

What are the two primary types of memory in a computer system, and what are their main functions?

Solution

- **RAM (Random Access Memory):** Volatile memory that temporarily stores active programs and data for fast access by the CPU.

- **ROM (Read-Only Memory):** Non-volatile memory that stores essential firmware and startup instructions, remaining intact even when power is off.

Problem 2 (Intermediate)

Question

Describe the basic structure of a computer system according to the Von Neumann architecture.

Solution

The Von Neumann architecture consists of a Central Processing Unit (CPU), a memory unit, and input/output devices connected via a system bus. The CPU processes instructions, memory temporarily or permanently stores data, and I/O devices facilitate user interaction. This unified architecture allows seamless communication among all components.

Problem 3 (Advanced)

Question

Compare the advantages of using SSDs over HDDs in modern computer systems.

Solution

- **Speed:** SSDs offer significantly faster read/write speeds due to the absence of moving parts.
- **Durability:** Without mechanical parts, SSDs are more resistant to physical shock and wear.
- **Power Consumption:** SSDs consume less power, resulting in better energy efficiency and longer battery life in portable devices.
- **Noise and Heat:** SSDs operate silently and generate less heat compared to HDDs, contributing to quieter and cooler systems.

Problem 4 (Challenging)

Question

Discuss how the integration of multi-core processors and advanced memory management techniques has transformed computing performance and multitasking capabilities over successive generations of personal computers.

Solution

- **Multi-Core Processors:** The evolution from single-core to multi-core CPUs has drastically increased processing power by allowing parallel execution of tasks, significantly improving multitasking and performance.
- **Advanced Memory Management:** Techniques such as dynamic memory allocation, paging, and virtual memory allow modern operating systems to efficiently allocate resources, reduce fragmentation, and manage multiple processes simultaneously.
- **Combined Impact:** Together, multi-core architectures and efficient memory management enable modern PCs to handle complex, resource-intensive

applications—from multimedia editing to large-scale data analytics—while maintaining stability and speed. This evolution has democratized computing, making robust systems accessible to both consumers and enterprises, and has paved the way for innovations like cloud computing, AI, and IoT.

1.3 PROCESSOR MODES AND MODERN CPU CONCEPTS

A processor, commonly known as the Central Processing Unit (CPU), operates in different modes to execute instructions efficiently. These modes determine how the CPU interacts with memory, hardware, and software components. Understanding processor modes is crucial for optimizing performance, ensuring security, and managing multitasking operations effectively.

Processor Modes

Modern CPUs operate in various modes that control execution privileges and system access. The three primary modes include Real Mode, Protected Mode, and Virtual Mode.

Real Mode

Real mode is the **most fundamental operational mode** of a processor, offering unrestricted access to memory and hardware resources. It is primarily used in early computing systems and legacy software environments.

- **Memory Access:** Limited to 1MB of memory due to 20-bit address lines.
- **Multitasking Support:** Not supported; only one process runs at a time.
- **Security:** No memory protection, leading to potential conflicts between programs.
- **Example Use Case:** Early DOS-based applications relied on real mode.

Protected Mode

Protected mode enhances the capabilities of a processor by introducing memory protection, multitasking, and virtual memory support. It allows modern operating systems to run efficiently.

- **Memory Access** Supports addressing beyond 1MB (up to 4GB or more, depending on the architecture).
- **Multitasking Support** Enables multiple applications to run simultaneously by managing CPU time allocation.
- **Security** Implements access controls, preventing unauthorized program execution.
- **Example Use Case** Modern operating systems such as Windows and Linux use protected mode for enhanced performance and security.

Virtual Mode

Virtual mode (Virtual 8086 mode) is a hybrid mode that enables a protected-mode operating system to run real-mode applications within a virtual environment.

- **Memory Access:** Uses virtual memory mapping to execute real-mode applications within a protected-mode OS.
- **Multitasking Support:** Allows multiple DOS applications to run simultaneously.
- **Security:** Each virtualized instance is isolated, preventing interference between running applications.

- **Example Use Case:** Legacy software requiring DOS compatibility operates in virtual mode within modern OS environments.

Modern CPU Concepts

With advancements in processor technology, modern CPUs incorporate multiple features that significantly improve computational power and efficiency.

Multi-Core Processors

Modern CPUs integrate multiple processing cores within a single chip, allowing **parallel execution of tasks**. This architecture enhances multitasking and computational performance.

Table 1.3 compares single-core and multi-core processors, emphasizing differences in speed, efficiency, multitasking capabilities, and power consumption. Multi-core processors provide higher performance and better multitasking while consuming **less power per core, making them more efficient for modern computing needs.

Table 1.3: *Comparison of Single-Core and Multi-Core Processors*

Feature	Single-Core Processor	Multi-Core Processor
Processing Speed	Limited	High
Efficiency	Low	High
Multitasking	Poor	Excellent
Power Consumption	Higher	Lower per Core

Hyper-Threading Technology (HTT)

Hyper-threading is Intel's proprietary technology that enables **simultaneous execution of multiple threads per core**, improving performance in multi-threaded applications.

- **Benefit:** Enhances CPU efficiency by keeping processor cores active even during idle cycles.
- **Use Case:** Useful in applications requiring high computational power, such as video editing and gaming.

Cache Memory and CPU Performance

Cache memory plays a critical role in **reducing latency** and speeding up processor data access. Modern CPUs have multiple cache levels:

Table 1.4: *Cache Memory Levels and Their Functions*

Cache Level	Location	Function
L1 Cache	Inside CPU Core	Stores frequently use instructions and data for quick access
L2 Cache	Separate but near CPU Core	Acts as a secondary cache for improved performance
L3 Cache	Shared across cores	Reduces bottlenecks in multi-core processors

Table 1.4 outlines the different cache memory levels, their locations, and their specific functions in improving CPU performance. L1 cache provides the fastest access to frequently used instructions, L2 cache serves as a secondary buffer, and L3 cache helps reduce bottlenecks in multi-core processors by sharing data among cores.

Overclocking and Performance Optimization

Overclocking refers to the practice of increasing a processor's clock speed beyond its factory settings to enhance performance. However, it comes with risks such as excessive heat generation and system instability.

- **Benefit:** Higher clock speeds improve processing power for demanding applications.
- **Risk:** Increased power consumption and thermal output require advanced cooling solutions.

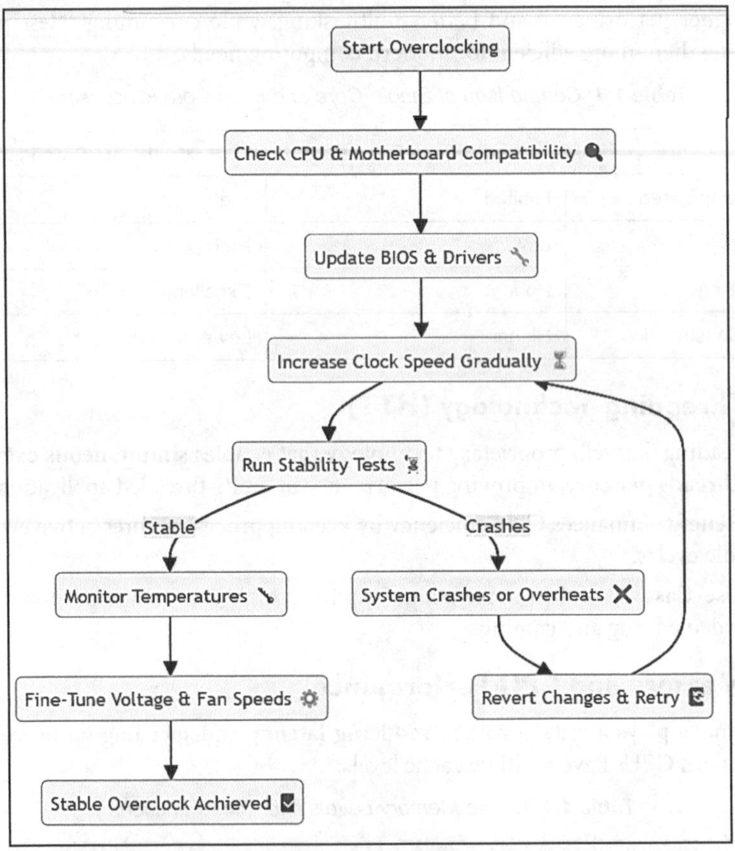

***Figure 1.3:** CPU Overclocking Process*

The following **Figure 1.3** illustrates the key steps involved in the process of CPU overclocking. It starts with checking hardware compatibility and updating BIOS, followed by gradually increasing clock speed while monitoring system stability and temperature. If the system remains stable, fine-tuning voltage and fan speeds ensures optimal performance. In case of instability, adjustments or reverting to previous settings may be necessary to prevent damage.

Conclusion

Processor modes define how a CPU interacts with system resources, ensuring efficient and secure execution of tasks. Modern CPUs incorporate multi-core architectures, hyper-threading, advanced caching mechanisms, and overclocking capabilities to optimize performance. Understanding these concepts is essential for designing and managing efficient computing systems.

Interesting Facts

- The first **Intel 8086 processor** introduced in **1978** operated in real mode.
- Modern processors can execute **billions of instructions per second**, thanks to **multi-core architectures**.
- **Overclocking** can improve CPU performance but significantly increases **heat output and power consumption**.
- **Hyper-threading** allows a single CPU core to **execute multiple threads simultaneously**, enhancing multitasking.

Processor Modes

Modern CPUs operate in various modes that control execution privileges and system access. The three primary modes include **Real Mode, Protected Mode, and Virtual Mode**.

Real Mode

Real mode is the most fundamental operational mode of a processor, offering unrestricted access to memory and hardware resources. It is primarily used in early computing systems and legacy software environments.

- **Memory Access:** Limited to **1MB of memory** due to 20-bit address lines.
- **Multitasking Support:** Not supported; only one process runs at a time.
- **Security:** No memory protection, leading to potential conflicts between programs.
- **Example Use Case:** Early DOS-based applications relied on real mode.

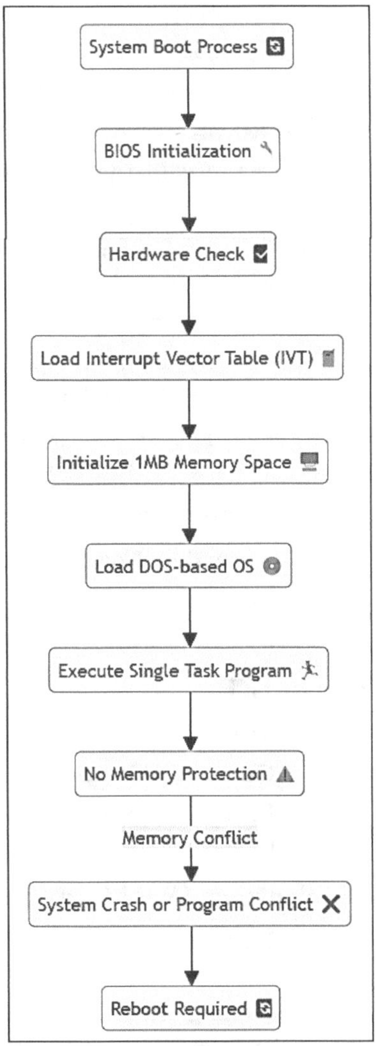

Figure 1.4: Real Mode Memory Structure

Figure 1.4 illustrates the step-by-step process of how a system operates in Real Mode. The flow begins with the system boot process, where the BIOS initializes and performs a hardware check. The Interrupt Vector Table (IVT) is then loaded, followed by memory initialization, which is restricted to 1MB due to the 20-bit address space. Once the DOS-based operating system is loaded, a single-task program executes. However, due to the lack of memory protection, memory conflicts can cause system crashes, requiring a reboot to recover.

Protected Mode

Protected mode enhances the capabilities of a processor by introducing memory protection, multitasking, and virtual memory support. It allows modern operating systems to run efficiently.

- **Memory Access:** Supports addressing beyond 1MB (up to 4GB or more, depending on the architecture).
- **Multitasking Support:** Enables multiple applications to run simultaneously by managing CPU time allocation.
- **Security:** Implements access controls, preventing unauthorized program execution.
- **Example Use Case:** Modern operating systems such as Windows and Linux use protected mode for enhanced performance and security.

Virtual Mode

Virtual mode (**Virtual 8086 mode**) is a hybrid mode that enables a protected-mode operating system to run real-mode applications within a virtual environment.

- **Memory Access:** Uses virtual memory mapping to execute real-mode applications within a protected-mode OS.
- **Multitasking Support:** Allows multiple DOS applications to run simultaneously.
- **Security:** Each virtualized instance is isolated, preventing interference between running applications.
- **Example Use Case:** Legacy software requiring **DOS compatibility** operates in virtual mode within modern OS environments.

Video Resources

- **Animation:** How CPU Modes Work
- Comparison of Processor Modes in Real-world Applications
- Demonstration of Overclocking Techniques and Performance Boosting

Use of ICT

- **Virtual Labs:** Simulating processor mode execution.
- **Online CPU Benchmarking Tools:** Analyzing real vs. protected mode efficiency.
- **Interactive Simulations:** Demonstrating multi-core and hyper-threading technology.

Applications (Real Life / Industrial)

- **Enterprise Computing:** High-end servers run in protected mode to ensure data security.
- **Gaming Industry:** Hyper-threading and multi-core CPUs optimize gaming performance.
- **Embedded Systems:** IoT devices operate in low-power CPU modes to enhance efficiency.

- **Cloud Computing:** Multi-threaded processors improve virtualization and cloud performance.

Case Study (Environmental/Sustainability Issues)

- **Power Consumption of High-Performance CPUs:** High-speed processors require advanced cooling and consume significant energy.
- **E-Waste from Upgraded CPUs:** Frequent processor upgrades contribute to global e-waste issues.
- **Green Computing Initiatives:** Companies like Intel and AMD develop energy-efficient CPUs for sustainability.

Create Inquisitiveness and Curiosity

- Why do some low-clock-speed CPUs outperform higher-clock-speed ones?
- How does quantum computing impact traditional CPU architecture?
- Can AI-based processors replace traditional CPUs?

Solved Problems (With Increasing Difficulty Level)

1. **Calculate CPU Execution Speed:** A processor has a clock speed of 3.2 GHz and executes four instructions per cycle. Determine the total instructions per second (IPS).
2. **Multi-Core Performance Analysis:** Given an 8-core CPU with 16 threads, calculate its theoretical speedup compared to a quad-core CPU.
3. **Thermal Considerations in Overclocking:** If a CPU has a TDP of 125W, determine the cooling requirement for safe overclocking.

SUMMARY

- Modern CPUs operate in real mode, protected mode, and virtual mode to handle different system requirements.
- Multi-core processors significantly improve performance and multitasking capabilities.
- Hyper-threading and cache memory enhance data processing speeds.
- Overclocking can boost CPU performance but requires proper cooling management.
- Advances in AI-driven and quantum processors will define the future of computing.

EXERCISES

1. Subjective Questions

1. Category-I (Revised Bloom's Level -1, 2 & 3)

1. Define real mode, protected mode, and virtual mode in processors.
2. Compare CISC and RISC architectures with examples.
3. Explain the role of clock speed and core count in CPU performance.

2. Category-II (Revised Bloom's Level -4, 5 & 6)

1. Analyze the impact of hyper-threading on multi-core CPUs.
2. Discuss how overclocking affects CPU longevity and system stability.

2. Objective Questions

1. Category-I (Revised Bloom's Level -1, 2 & 3)

1. What is the primary advantage of **multi-core processors?**
   (a) Increased cache memory (b) Higher clock speed
   ((c) Improved parallel processing ((d) Reduced voltage requirements
2. Which of the following processor architectures is **used in most smartphones?**
   (a) x86 (b) ARM
   ((c) RISC-V ((d) CISC

Category-II (Revised Bloom's Level -4, 5 & 6)

1. How does thread scheduling in modern CPUs enhance performance?
2. What are the security vulnerabilities associated with processor overclocking?

TEACHER'S KNOW MORE

- **The Evolution of Processor Modes:** How early CPUs evolved from single-mode execution to multi-core operations.
- **CPU Security Mechanisms:** The role of hardware-level encryption and secure enclaves in modern processors.
- **Emerging Trends in CPU Design:** AI-based CPUs and quantum processing units (QPUs).
- **Industry Case Studies:** Performance benchmarks of Intel Core i9 vs AMD Ryzen 9 in real-world applications.

1.4 ESSENTIAL MEMORY CONCEPTS

Memory is a fundamental component of any computer system, responsible for storing and retrieving data efficiently. The performance and functionality of a computer system depend significantly on the type, speed, and management of memory.

Types of Memory

Memory in a computer is categorized into two main types: Primary Memory (Volatile Memory) and Secondary Memory (Non-Volatile Memory).

Primary Memory (Volatile Memory)

Primary memory, also known as main memory, temporarily holds data and instructions required by the CPU during execution. When the system is powered off, the data stored in this memory is lost. The two primary types of volatile memory are Random Access Memory (RAM) and Cache Memory.

Random Access Memory (RAM)

RAM is the primary working memory of a computer that stores active programs and data. It enables quick read and write operations, significantly affecting system performance.

- **Dynamic RAM (DRAM):** Requires constant refreshing to maintain data and is commonly used in main system memory.
- **Static RAM (SRAM):** Faster than DRAM as it does not need frequent refreshing. Used in cache memory for high-speed data access.

Cache Memory

Cache memory is a high-speed memory located closer to the processor, designed to store frequently accessed data to improve processing speed. Modern CPUs implement multiple levels of cache. **Table 1.5** presents the Cache Memory Hierarchy, detailing the levels, their locations, speeds, and functions in optimizing CPU performance. The L1 cache is the fastest and stores frequently accessed instructions. The L2 cache acts as an intermediate buffer, and the L3 cache, though slower, enhances multi-core efficiency by reducing bottlenecks.

Table 1.5: *Cache Memory Hierarchy: Levels, Speed, and Functions*

Cache Level	Location	Speed	Function
L1 Cache	Inside CPU Core	Fastest	Stores frequently accessed instructions
L2 Cache	Near CPU Core	Fast	Holds additional temporary data
L3 Cache	Shared among cores	Moderate	Reduces bottlenecks in multi-core processors

Figure 1.5 illustrates the hierarchical structure of cache memory in modern processors. The L1 cache, located inside the CPU core, is the fastest and stores frequently accessed instructions. The L2 cache, positioned near the CPU core, serves as an additional buffer, providing high-speed data access. The L3 cache is shared among multiple cores to help reduce data bottlenecks in multi-core processors. Beyond cache memory, RAM (main memory) stores active data, while storage (SSD/HD(d) holds long-term data. The hierarchical design ensures efficient data retrieval, optimizing processing speed and system performance.

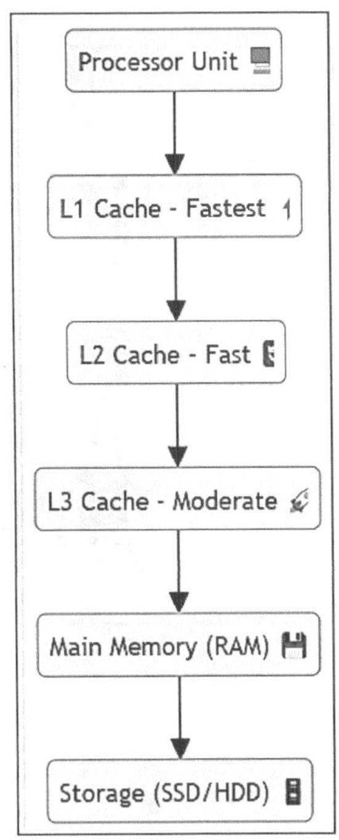

Figure 1.5: *Cache Memory Hierarchy*

Secondary Memory (Non-Volatile Memory)

Secondary memory provides long-term data storage, allowing users to save files and system configurations even when the computer is turned off.

Read-Only Memory (ROM)

ROM is a non-volatile memory that permanently stores essential firmware required for system booting and hardware initialization.

- **Programmable ROM (PROM):** Can be written once and retains data permanently.
- **Erasable PROM (EPROM):** Can be erased using ultraviolet light and reprogrammed.

- **Electrically Erasable PROM (EEPROM):** It can be erased and reprogrammed electronically and is widely used in modern firmware updates.

Hard Disk Drives (HD(d) and Solid-State Drives (SSD)

The most common secondary storage devices include **HDDs** and **SSDs.** HDDs use spinning magnetic disks for data storage, while SSDs use flash memory, offering faster read/write speeds and improved durability. **Table 1.6** compares HDD and SSD storage technologies, highlighting their differences in speed, durability, cost, and power consumption. SSDs provide faster performance, more outstanding durability, and lower power consumption, while HDDs remain a more economical option with higher storage capacity per dollar.

Table 1.6: *Comparison of HDD and SSD Storage Technologies*

Feature	HDD	SSD
Speed	Slower	Faster
Durability	Mechanical Parts	No Moving Parts
Price	Economical	Expensive
Power Consumption	Higher	Lower

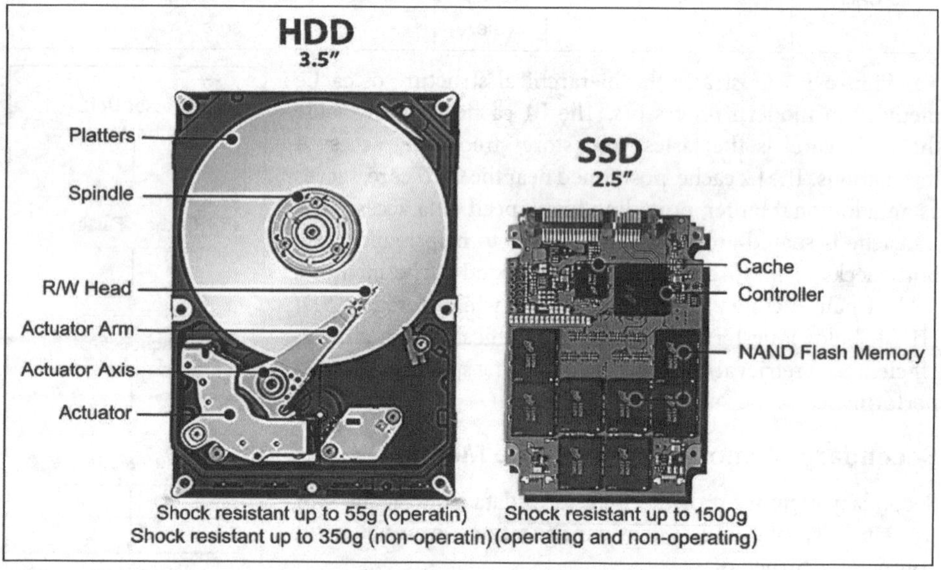

Figure 1.6: *HDD vs SSD Comparison*

Figure 1.6 illustrates the key differences between Hard Disk Drives (HDDs) and Solid State Drives (SSDs). HDDs rely on mechanical components, including spinning platters and a read/write head, to store and retrieve data, making them slower and more susceptible to physical damage. SSDs, in contrast, use NAND flash memory, eliminating moving parts and significantly improving read and write speeds. HDDs offer large storage capacities at a lower cost, but their mechanical nature results in higher latency and power consumption. SSDs, while more expensive per gigabyte, provide superior durability, energy efficiency, and overall system responsiveness. The shock resistance of SSDs is much higher, making them ideal for modern computing environments where speed and reliability are critical.

Memory Management and Optimization

Memory management is essential for optimizing system performance and preventing memory-related issues. The operating system efficiently manages memory allocation and deallocation through several techniques.

- **Virtual Memory:** Extends physical RAM by using storage as temporary memory when RAM is full, allowing multitasking.
- **Memory Paging:** Divides memory into fixed-sized pages to enhance data retrieval efficiency.
- **Segmentation:** Allocates memory in variable-sized segments to improve system responsiveness.
- **Garbage Collection:** Frees unused memory in programming environments to prevent memory leaks.

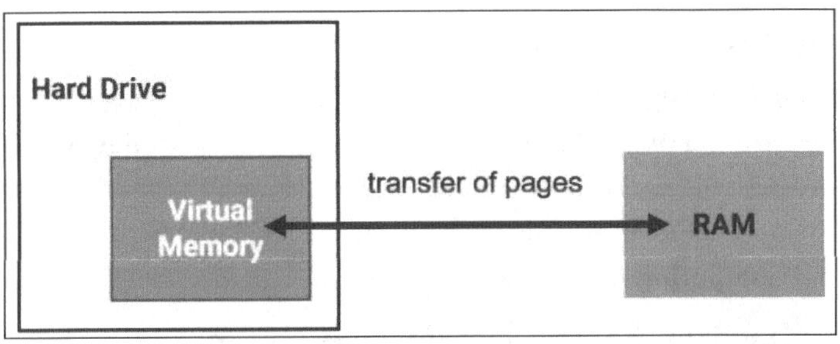

Figure 1.7: *Virtual Memory Process*

Figure 1.7 illustrates the Virtual Memory Process, demonstrating how a computer utilizes storage space to extend its physical memory capacity. When the system runs out of available RAM, it moves less frequently accessed data to a designated portion of the hard drive or SSD, known as virtual memory or a paging file.

This allows the computer to handle more applications than the RAM alone could support. However, because accessing virtual memory from storage is significantly slower than accessing RAM, excessive reliance on it can reduce system performance. Efficient memory management, such as increasing physical RAM or optimizing software usage, helps minimize the need for virtual memory, ensuring a smoother computing experience.

Understanding memory concepts is crucial for efficient system performance and application execution. Modern computing relies on efficient memory hierarchies and management techniques to optimize speed and reduce latency.

Interesting Facts

- The first DRAM (Dynamic RAM) chip was invented in 1968, revolutionizing modern computing.
- Cache memory is significantly faster than RAM, reducing data access time for the CPU.
- SSD storage is up to 100 times faster than traditional HDDs, improving overall system performance.
- Some supercomputers use non-volatile memory (NVM) instead of traditional RAM to enhance efficiency.

Video Resources

- **How Cache Memory Works**: Understanding CPU Cache Architecture.
- **Difference Between RAM and Virtual Memory**: Explains memory allocation techniques.
- **Comparing HDD vs SSD Performance**: Benchmarking storage devices.

Use of ICT

- **Virtual Labs:** Simulating RAM and Cache memory access speeds.
- **Memory Allocation Simulations:** Demonstrating memory paging and segmentation.
- **Interactive Storage Benchmarking Tools:** Comparing HDD and SSD performance.

Applications (Real Life / Industrial)

- **Gaming PCs:** High-speed RAM and VRAM improve gaming performance.
- **Enterprise Servers:** Use of ECC (Error Correcting Code) memory for data integrity.
- **IoT Devices:** Low-power memory for smart homes and wearables.
- **Cloud Computing:** Virtual memory allocation enhances cloud-based applications.

Case Study (Environmental/Sustainability Issues)

- **E-Waste from Discarded Memory Modules:** Growing disposal of outdated RAM and storage devices contributes to environmental concerns.
- **Innovations in Biodegradable Storage:** Research into biodegradable circuit boards and memory chips.
- **Energy-Efficient Memory Solutions:** Development of low-power DRAM and memory to reduce power consumption.

Create Inquisitiveness and Curiosity

- Can DNA-based memory storage replace RAM in the future?
- Why do SSDs perform better than HDDs despite having no moving parts?
- How does memory bandwidth affect system performance?

Solved Problems (With Increasing Difficulty Level)

1. **Calculate Memory Bandwidth:** If a DDR4 RAM operates at 3200 MHz with a 64-bit bus, determine its theoretical transfer rate.
2. **Compare Read/Write Speeds:** Given an HDD (100 MB/s) and SSD (500 MB/s), calculate the time required to transfer a 10GB file.
3. **Virtual Memory Calculation:** If a system has 8GB RAM and a 16GB page file, what is the total available memory?

SUMMARY

- Primary memory (RAM, Cache) is fast but volatile, while secondary memory (ROM, HDD, SS(d) is non-volatile.

- Cache memory reduces latency and accelerates CPU operations.
- Virtual memory and paging improve multitasking and system efficiency.
- SSDs outperform HDDs in terms of speed, durability, and power consumption.
- Future trends include AI-optimized memory management and quantum storage solutions.

EXERCISES

1. Subjective Questions

Category-I (Revised Bloom's Level -1, 2 & 3)

1. Explain the differences between RAM, ROM, and Cache Memory.
2. Compare the advantages of SSD over HDD.
3. Describe the function of Virtual Memory in system performance.

Category-II (Revised Bloom's Level -4, 5 & 6)

1. Analyze how memory bandwidth affects system performance.
2. Discuss the role of cache hierarchy in CPU performance.

1.5 SELECTING AND INSTALLING MEMORY

Memory selection and installation play a crucial role in optimizing system performance. Choosing the correct type of memory ensures that a computer operates efficiently, handles workloads effectively, and prevents bottlenecks in processing speeds. The process involves understanding various memory types, compatibility factors, and installation procedures.

Understanding RAM Specifications

When selecting RAM, several specifications determine its suitability for a computer system. These include memory type, speed, capacity, and latency.

- **Memory Type:** The most common types are **DDR3, DDR4, and DDR5**. Each generation improves bandwidth, energy efficiency, and processing speed.
- **Memory Speed (MHz):** The clock speed of RAM, measured in megahertz (MHz), determines how fast data is processed. Higher speeds result in better performance, particularly in multitasking and gaming environments.
- **Capacity:** RAM capacity is measured in gigabytes (G(b). For basic computing, **4GB to 8GB** is sufficient, while professional applications and gaming require **16GB or more.**
- **CAS Latency:** This refers to the delay between memory request and data retrieval. Lower latency values improve system response times.

Compatibility Factors

Selecting the right RAM for a system requires considering **compatibility with the motherboard and processor**. Key factors include:

- **Motherboard Memory Slots:** Different motherboards support specific types and configurations of RAM. Checking the motherboard's **specification manual** ensures compatibility.

- **Dual-Channel vs. Quad-Channel Memory:** Memory channels affect data transfer rates. Dual-channel memory improves performance by allowing simultaneous data transmission across two memory modules.
- **Voltage Requirements:** Modern RAM modules operate at lower voltages for better energy efficiency. For instance, **DDR4 operates at 1.2V**, while **DDR5 operates at 1.1V**.

Installing RAM Modules

Proper installation of memory modules is essential for system stability and performance. The installation process involves the following steps:

1. **Power Down the System:** Shut down the computer and disconnect the power supply to prevent electrical damage.
2. **Access the Motherboard:** Open the computer case and locate the **DIMM slots** on the motherboard.
3. **Align the RAM Module:** Ensure the module's notch matches the slot key, preventing incorrect insertion.
4. **Insert the Module:** Firmly press the RAM into the slot until the side clips lock it in place.
5. **Power On and Verify:** Restart the system and check memory recognition through BIOS or system properties.

Figure 1.8 illustrates the RAM Installation Process, demonstrating how a memory module is inserted into a motherboard's DIMM (Dual In-line Memory Module) slot. Proper RAM installation is crucial for enhancing system performance by increasing memory capacity.The RAM module must be aligned with the notch on the slot to ensure a correct fit and gentle pressure is applied until the side clips snap into place, securing the module. Before installation, it is essential to power off the system and discharge any static electricity to prevent hardware damage. Once installed, the system can utilize the additional memory to improve multitasking capabilities and overall processing speed.

Figure 1.8: RAM Installation Process

Common Memory Installation Issues and Troubleshooting

- **System Fails to Boot:** Ensure that the RAM module is seated correctly and compatible with the motherboard.
- **Frequent Crashes or Blue Screen Errors:** Check for BIOS updates and adjust memory configurations.
- **Lower Than Expected Memory Capacity Detected:** Verify that the operating system supports the installed RAM amount (e.g., 32-bit OS supports only 4GB RAM).

Efficient memory selection and installation are essential for achieving peak system performance. Understanding RAM specifications, compatibility, and installation techniques ensures a smooth computing experience while minimizing hardware issues.

Interesting Facts

- The first RAM module, developed in 1968, could store only 1 KB of data.
- DDR5 RAM provides higher bandwidth and lower power consumption compared to DDR4.
- Most modern gaming PCs use at least 16GB of RAM for optimal performance.
- Laptops with soldered RAM cannot be upgraded, unlike desktop systems.

Video Resources

- **Step-by-Step RAM Installation Guide:** Demonstrates memory installation techniques.
- **DDR3 vs. DDR4 vs. DDR5 Performance Comparison:** Understanding the impact of different RAM types.
- **How to Troubleshoot RAM Issues:** Identifying and fixing memory-related problems.

Use of ICT

- **Virtual Simulations:** Demonstrating RAM installation procedures.
- **Memory Benchmarking Tools:** Comparing performance improvements with different RAM configurations.
- **Online Configuration Tools:** Checking motherboard RAM compatibility.

Applications (Real Life/Industrial)

- **Gaming Systems:** High-speed RAM enhances FPS and game responsiveness.
- **Data Centers:** Enterprise servers require high-capacity and ECC memory for reliable computing.
- **Graphic Design & Video Editing:** Higher RAM capacity speeds up rendering and processing times.
- **AI and Machine Learning:** Large datasets require optimized RAM for efficient processing.

Case Study (Environmental/Sustainability Issues)

- **E-Waste from Upgrading RAM:** Old memory modules contribute to **electronic waste**, requiring proper recycling.
- **Energy Efficiency of DDR5:** Newer RAM consumes less power, reducing the carbon footprint of computing.
- **Future of Memory Technology:** Emerging optane and quantum memory solutions promise higher efficiency and sustainability.

Create Inquisitiveness and Curiosity

- How does RAM speed affect gaming performance?
- Why do some computers support only specific RAM types?
- What are the benefits of upgrading RAM vs. upgrading storage?

Solved Problems (With Increasing Difficulty Level)

1. **Calculate Data Transfer Speed:** A DDR4 module operates at 3200 MHz with a 64-bit bus. Determine its data transfer rate.
2. **Memory Channel Performance Analysis:** Compare single-channel vs. dual-channel memory performance in real-world applications.
3. **Troubleshooting RAM Compatibility Issues:** A user installs DDR4 RAM in a DDR3 motherboard. Explain why it fails and suggest solutions.

SUMMARY

- Selecting the right RAM involves considering type, speed, and compatibility.
- Installing RAM correctly ensures optimal system performance and stability.
- Newer RAM generations (DDR5) improve efficiency, power consumption, and performance.
- Troubleshooting memory issues is crucial for ensuring system reliability.
- Future memory technologies like quantum and optane memory will redefine computing performance.

EXERCISES

1. Subjective Questions

Category-I (Revised Bloom's Level -1, 2 & 3)

1. Explain the differences between DDR3, DDR4, and DDR5 RAM.
2. Describe the step-by-step procedure to install a RAM module.
3. What factors should be considered when selecting RAM for a high-performance system?

Category-II (Revised Bloom's Level -4, 5 & 6)

1. Analyze the advantages of dual-channel vs. quad-channel memory configurations.
2. Discuss the impact of memory latency on CPU performance.

1.6 COOLING MECHANISMS FOR CPUS AND MEMORY

Efficient cooling mechanisms are essential for maintaining optimal system performance and prolonging hardware lifespan. Excess heat can cause performance degradation, system instability, and hardware failures. To prevent these issues, modern computers employ various cooling solutions to regulate temperature and ensure smooth operation.

Importance of Cooling Systems

CPUs and memory modules generate heat due to continuous data processing and electrical activity. Without proper cooling, high temperatures can lead to thermal throttling, where the processor reduces its clock speed to prevent overheating. Additionally, prolonged exposure to excessive heat can damage components and lead to premature hardware failure. Cooling systems not only enhance system stability and efficiency but also enable safe overclocking, allowing users to push hardware performance beyond factory settings without compromising reliability.

Types of Cooling Systems

1. Air Cooling

Air cooling is the most commonly used method due to its cost-effectiveness and simplicity. It relies on heat sinks and fans to dissipate heat away from components.

Figure 1.9: *Liquid Cooling System*

- **Heat Sinks:** Made of aluminium or copper, these passive cooling components absorb heat from the CPU or memory and transfer it away through **thermal conduction**.
- **Cooling Fans:** Active cooling components that enhance heat dissipation by increasing airflow over the heat sink and surrounding areas.
- **Case Fans:** Positioned inside the computer case to regulate airflow, preventing heat buildup.

Figure 9 illustrates a Liquid Cooling System, a high-performance cooling solution designed to regulate CPU temperatures efficiently. Unlike traditional air cooling, which relies on heat sinks and fans, liquid cooling uses a closed-loop system with coolant circulated through tubes to transfer heat away from the processor. The system consists of a water block, which absorbs heat from the CPU, tubing that carries the heated coolant to a radiator, and fans that dissipate the heat. Liquid cooling is particularly effective for overclocked or high-performance gaming PCs, as it provides better thermal management, reduces noise levels, and enhances system longevity by preventing overheating.

2. Liquid Cooling

For high-performance computing, liquid cooling offers superior thermal management compared to air cooling. It utilizes a closed-loop system with coolant circulating through tubes to dissipate heat.

- **Water Blocks:** Installed over the CPU and memory modules to absorb heat.
- **Radiators and Pumps:** The heated coolant passes through a radiator, where fans help dissipate the heat before recirculating it back.
- **Coolant Liquid:** Special non-conductive fluids that transfer heat efficiently without damaging electronic components.

Liquid cooling is ideal for gaming PCs, workstations, and overclocking setups, where heat dissipation demands are high.

3. Phase-change and Advanced Cooling Solutions

For extreme performance applications, advanced cooling technologies like phase-change cooling and thermoelectric cooling are used.

- **Phase-Change Cooling:** Similar to refrigeration, where a compressed liquid absorbs heat and evaporates to cool the CPU.
- **Peltier Coolers (Thermoelectric Coolers - TECs):** Generate a temperature differential using electrical current to cool components efficiently.

- **Submersion Cooling:** This involves submerging hardware components in non-conductive cooling fluids for enhanced thermal performance.

These methods are used in data centres and specialized high-performance computing (HP(c) environments where heat management is critical.

Cooling Considerations for Memory Modules

Memory modules also generate heat, especially high-performance RAM used in gaming and overclocking. Passive and active cooling solutions for RAM include:

- **Heat Spreaders:** Metal plates attached to memory modules to improve heat dissipation.
- **Dedicated RAM Cooling Fans:** Small fans mounted on memory slots to regulate temperature.
- **Water-Cooled RAM Modules:** Custom liquid cooling loops designed for memory-intensive applications.

Best Practices for Thermal Management

To ensure an efficient cooling system, follow these best practices:

- **Apply Thermal Paste Properly:** Ensures optimal contact between the CPU and the heat sink for maximum heat transfer.
- **Maintain Good Airflow:** Proper positioning of case fans helps direct hot air out and cool air in.
- **Regular Cleaning:** Dust accumulation on heat sinks and fans reduces cooling efficiency. Cleaning prevents overheating.
- **Monitor Temperatures:** Use hardware monitoring software to track CPU and memory temperatures.

Conclusion

Cooling mechanisms are an essential aspect of maintaining system performance and hardware longevity. Proper cooling solutions, whether air-based or liquid-based, ensure efficient heat dissipation, enabling processors and memory to function optimally. By following **best practices in thermal management**, users can prevent overheating issues and maximize the lifespan of their hardware.

Interesting Facts

- The first CPU cooling fan was introduced in the early 1990s to prevent overheating.
- Liquid cooling can reduce temperatures by 30% more efficiently than air cooling.
- Thermal throttling reduces CPU speed automatically to prevent overheating and hardware damage.
- Some high-performance gaming PCs use submersion cooling, where components are submerged in a non-conductive liquid.

Video Resources

- **How Air and Liquid Cooling Work**: A comparison of different cooling solutions.
- **Overclocking and Its Impact on Cooling**: Understanding temperature management during overclocking.
- **Building a Liquid-Cooled PC**: Step-by-step guide on installing liquid cooling.

Use of ICT

- **Virtual Simulations:** Demonstrating heat dissipation in different cooling systems.
- **Temperature Monitoring Software:** Analyzing real-time CPU temperature under different loads.
- **Overclocking Benchmarks:** Measuring performance and temperature variations in overclocked CPUs.

Applications (Real Life / Industrial)

- **Gaming Rigs:** Liquid cooling is widely used in high-performance gaming PCs to prevent thermal throttling.
- **Data Centers: Phase-change cooling** helps maintain optimal temperatures in large-scale data centres.
- **Medical Imaging Devices:** High-performance CPUs in MRI and CT scanners require efficient cooling to avoid overheating.
- **Automotive Electronics:** Engine control units (ECUs) use specialized cooling mechanisms for continuous processing.

Case Study (Environmental/Sustainability Issues)

- **Heat Dissipation and Energy Waste:** Data centres generate enormous heat, increasing energy consumption and cooling costs.
- **Eco-Friendly Cooling Systems:** Liquid immersion cooling reduces energy use by eliminating the need for fans.
- **Recycling and Reusing Heat:** Some industries reuse excess heat from servers to power other operations, reducing waste.

Create Inquisitiveness and Curiosity

- Why do high-performance processors require better cooling?
- Can biodegradable coolants replace traditional liquid cooling solutions?
- What are the long-term effects of heat on CPU lifespan?

Solved Problems

1. **Thermal Conductivity Calculation:** A heat sink transfers 100W of heat with a thermal resistance of 0.3°C/W. Determine the CPU temperature increase.
2. **Cooling System Efficiency:** Compare the heat dissipation efficiency of a liquid cooling system vs. an air-cooled system.
3. **Overclocking Temperature Analysis:** If a CPU is overclocked from 3.5 GHz to 4.5 GHz, how much additional cooling capacity is needed?

SUMMARY

- Cooling systems prevent overheating and thermal throttling, ensuring system stability.
- Air cooling and liquid cooling are the most common cooling methods.
- Advanced cooling solutions like phase-change and submersion cooling are used in HPC and data centres.

- Memory cooling solutions ensure high-performance RAM stability.
- Proper thermal management extends hardware lifespan and enhances computing efficiency.

EXERCISES

1. Subjective Questions

Category-I (Revised Bloom's Level -1, 2 & 3)

1. Explain the working principles of heat sinks and cooling fans.
2. Compare air cooling vs. liquid cooling.
3. What are the benefits of applying thermal paste during CPU installation?

Category-II (Revised Bloom's Level -4, 5 & 6)

1. Analyze how temperature affects CPU performance.
2. Discuss the future of cooling technologies in high-performance computing.

SUMMARY

This unit provided an in-depth exploration of the fundamental concepts related to **Personal Computers (PCs) and Memory**. The topics covered include:

- **Evolution of Personal Computers:** A historical overview, starting from mechanical computing devices to modern high-performance systems.
- **Overview of Systems and Components:** Understanding of key components such as the CPU, Memory, Storage, Input/Output devices, Motherboard, and Power Supply.
- **Processor Modes and Modern CPU Concepts:** Discussion on Real Mode, Protected Mode, and Virtual Mode, as well as multi-core processors, hyper-threading, and cache memory.
- **Essential Memory Concepts:** Explanation of RAM, ROM, Cache Memory, and their importance in system performance.
- **Selecting and Installing Memory:** Guidelines on choosing memory based on **type, speed, capacity, and compatibility**, along with proper installation techniques.
- **Cooling Mechanisms for CPUs and Memory:** Various air, liquid, and advanced cooling solutions are used to maintain system stability and performance.

EXERCISES

1. Subjective Questions

1. Explain the evolution of personal computers, highlighting the major technological advancements from first-generation to modern computing.
2. Describe the key components of a computer system and their roles in executing computing tasks.

3. Compare and contrast Real Mode, Protected Mode, and Virtual Mode of CPU operation.
4. Differentiate between volatile and non-volatile memory, providing examples of each.
5. Discuss the importance of cache memory and its impact on CPU performance.
6. Outline the steps involved in selecting and installing RAM in a computer system.
7. Compare air cooling and liquid cooling in terms of efficiency, cost, and suitability for different computing environments.
8. What are the benefits and risks associated with overclocking a CPU?
9. Explain how memory management techniques such as virtual memory and paging improve system performance.
10. Describe best practices for maintaining an efficient cooling system in a high-performance PC setup.

2. Multiple-Choice Questions (MCQs)

1. Which of the following memory types is **non-volatile**?
   (a) RAM (b) ROM
   (c) Cache Memory (d) DRAM
2. The primary function of the CPU's Control Unit (CU) is to:
   (a) Perform arithmetic operations (b) Manage input and output devices
   (c) Direct the execution of instructions (d) Store frequently accessed data
3. Which CPU mode allows multitasking and memory protection?
   (a) Real Mode (b) Protected Mode
   (c) Virtual Mode (d) User Mode
4. Cache memory is used to:
   (a) Store the operating system permanently
   (b) Provide additional space for file storage
   (c) Temporarily store frequently accessed data for faster retrieval
   (d) Increase the physical RAM size
5. The main advantage of solid-state drives (SSDs) over hard disk drives (HDDs) is:
   (a) Higher storage capacity (b) Lower cost
   (c) Faster data read/write speeds (d) Greater mechanical durability

3. True or False

1. The Von Neumann architecture is the foundation of modern computing. *(True/False)*
2. DDR5 RAM operates at a higher voltage than DDR4 RAM. *(True/False)*
3. Heat sinks are only used in liquid cooling systems. *(True/False)*
4. BIOS firmware is stored in volatile memory. *(True/False)*
5. L1 cache memory is faster than L3 cache memory. *(True/False)*

TEACHER'S KNOW MORE

For further exploration, educators and students can:

- Refer to advanced readings on processor architecture and memory hierarchy.
- Conducted hands-on experiments on RAM installation and BIOS configuration.
- Explore industry case studies on high-performance computing and liquid cooling applications.

2

MOTHERBOARD DESIGNS

UNIT

RATIONALE

Modern computing relies heavily on the design and functionality of motherboards, which serve as the backbone connecting all components of a computer system. This unit is designed to provide learners with an in-depth understanding of various motherboard form factors, components, chipsets, and connectivity options. By studying the evolution—from early designs like IBM PC XT/AT to modern ATX variations—and exploring components like expansion slots, BIOS/UEFI firmware, and connectivity upgrades, students will:

- **Develop a Technical Foundation:** Gain critical insights into how different motherboard designs affect system performance, scalability, and upgradeability.
- **Enhance Problem-Solving Skills:** Learn to choose the appropriate motherboard based on specific use cases, balancing factors like form factor, compatibility, and connectivity.
- **Prepare for Real-World Applications:** Understand industry trends and design principles that drive modern computer architectures, which is essential for careers in IT, hardware engineering, and systems design.
- **Promote Innovation:** Inspire creative thinking about future motherboard technologies and customization options, such as RGB lighting and advanced connectivity features.

This unit not only lays the groundwork for advanced hardware knowledge but also encourages the application of these principles in designing, upgrading, and troubleshooting computer systems in various real-world scenarios.

OUTCOMES

By the end of this unit, students will be able to:

- **Identify and Differentiate Motherboard Form Factors:**
  - Recognize historical and modern motherboard designs (e.g., IBM PC XT, Baby AT, ATX, Micro-ATX, NLX) and understand their respective use cases.
- **Explain Key Motherboard Components and Expansion Slots:**
  - Describe the differences between active and passive motherboards.
  - Identify various components such as CPU sockets and DIMM.2, M.2, and PCIe Gen3 M.2 expansion cards.
  - Discuss compatibility issues, for instance, with models like the Intel D850GB.
- **Understand Chipsets and Firmware Integration:**
  - Compare Intel versus non-Intel chipsets and explain the roles of North Bridge and South Bridge.
  - Detail the functions of CMOS, BIOS, and UEFI firmware and their impact on system configuration and performance.
  - Explain how features like RGB headers contribute to motherboard customization.

- **Evaluate Connectivity Options and Upgrade Strategies:**
  - Analyze next-generation connectivity features (e.g., 802.11 AD WiFi, USB 3.1 Gen2) and how they enhance system performance.
  - Outline best practices for upgrading motherboards, including memory support like DDR4 BOOST and the integration of modern display solutions like Live Dash OLED.
- **Apply Knowledge to Real-World Scenarios:**
  - Recommend the appropriate motherboard design for different computing needs, considering factors like form factor, expansion capabilities, and future upgrade potential.
  - Develop troubleshooting strategies and upgrade plans based on a detailed understanding of motherboard components and technologies.

2.1 MOTHERBOARD FORM FACTORS

The **motherboard** is the central circuit board that connects and allows communication between all components of a computer system. It serves as the foundation for hardware integration, providing slots for the processor, memory, storage, and peripheral devices. Different motherboard form factors exist to cater to varying system requirements, including **size, expansion capabilities, and power consumption.**

IBM PC XT and IBM PC AT

The IBM PC XT (eXtended Technology) and IBM PC AT (Advanced Technology) were among the earliest personal computer motherboards. The XT motherboard was introduced in 1983 with **8-bit expansion slots**, while the AT motherboard, introduced in 1984, supported **16-bit expansion slots** and larger memory capacities. These designs set the groundwork for modern motherboard architectures.

Baby AT Form Factor

The Baby AT motherboard was a compact version of the IBM AT motherboard. Introduced in the late 1980s, it maintained compatibility with the AT standard but reduced overall size to improve space efficiency within computer cases.

Key Features

- Smaller dimensions compared to AT motherboards
- Used **5-pin DIN connectors** for keyboards
- Supported **AT-style power connectors**
- Predecessor to the ATX form factor

ATX (Advanced Technology eXtende(d)

The ATX form factor, introduced by Intel in 1995, became the industry standard due to its enhanced layout and improved airflow design. It features integrated I/O ports, a standard power supply connection, and increased expansion slot support.

Key Features

- Standard size: **305mm × 244mm (12 × 9.6 inches)**
- Supports **up to seven expansion slots**
- It uses **24-pin power connectors** for stable power delivery
- Improves **cable management and component accessibility**

Micro-ATX and Mini-ATX

Micro-ATX and Mini-ATX motherboards are **smaller variations** of the ATX standard, designed for compact and budget-friendly systems.

Table 2.1: *Comparison of Micro-ATX and Mini-ATX Motherboard Form Factors*

Feature	Micro-ATX	Mini-ATX
Size	244mm × 244mm	284mm × 208mm
Expansion Slots	Up to 4	Up to 3
Power Connector	24-pin ATX	24-pin ATX
Suitable For	Budget and mid-range PCs	Small form-factor builds

Table 2.1 compares the Micro-ATX and Mini-ATX motherboard form factors, focusing on size, expansion capabilities, power requirements, and suitability. Micro-ATX offers more expansion slots and is ideal for budget and mid-range PCs, whereas Mini-ATX is designed for compact, small form-factor builds.

LPX (Low Profile extension) and Mini-LPX

LPX motherboards were used in compact desktop cases during the 1990s. They featured **riser cards**, which allowed horizontal expansion cards to be installed, reducing overall height.

Mini-LPX was a reduced version of LPX designed for space-constrained systems.

NLX (New Low Profile eXtende(d)

The NLX motherboard was an improvement over LPX, with support for **better airflow, tool-free component installation, and improved expansion slot accessibility.** It was commonly used in corporate desktop computers.

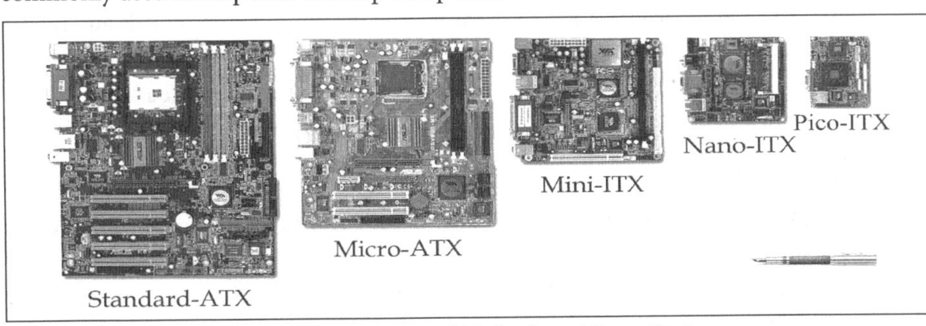

Figure 2.1: *Evolution of Motherboard Form Factors*

Figure 2.1 illustrates the Evolution of Motherboard Form Factors, showcasing various sizes and their applications in computing.

- **Standard-ATX**: The largest among the shown form factors, commonly used in gaming PCs and workstations, offering multiple expansion slots and high performance.
- **Micro-ATX**: A **compact** version of ATX, balancing performance and space efficiency, often used in mid-range desktops.

- **Mini-ITX**: A smaller form factor designed for compact builds, such as HTPCs (Home Theater PCs) and small form factor gaming PCs, with limited expansion slots.
- **Nano-ITX**: Primarily used in embedded systems and industrial applications, with a focus on low power consumption.
- **Pico-ITX**: The smallest among them, suitable for IoT devices, robotics, and embedded computing, where space and power efficiency are critical.

As motherboard form factors evolve, they cater to different computing needs, from high-performance desktops to miniature, power-efficient embedded systems, enabling advancements in PC customization and miniaturization.

Choosing the Right Motherboard

Selecting the appropriate motherboard depends on several factors:

- **System Purpose:** Gaming, workstation, or office use
- **Expansion Needs:** Number of PCIe slots and RAM support
- **Power Delivery:** Compatibility with high-performance processors
- **Connectivity:** USB, SATA, and NVMe support

Motherboards have evolved significantly, with modern designs integrating **Wi-Fi modules, enhanced power efficiency, and AI-based performance optimizations.** The following section explores the **components and expansion slots of a motherboard**, highlighting their impact on overall system functionality.

Interesting Facts

- The first personal computer motherboard was developed by IBM in 1981.
- ATX motherboards, introduced in 1995, are still widely used today due to their modularity and expandability.
- Mini-ITX motherboards are commonly used in compact gaming PCs and media centres.
- Modern motherboards integrate Wi-Fi, Bluetooth, and high-speed USB-C ports for seamless connectivity.

Video Resources

- **The Evolution of Motherboard Form Factors**: A historical overview of different motherboard types.
- **How to Choose the Right Motherboard for our PC Build**: Guide on selecting form factors.
- **Micro-ATX vs ATX: Which Should We Choose?**: Performance and expansion slot comparison.

Use of ICT

- **Virtual Labs:** Simulating motherboard form factor configurations.
- **3D Motherboard Explorer:** Interactive analysis of components and connections.
- **Motherboard Benchmarking Tools:** Comparing ATX, Micro-ATX, and Mini-ITX performance.

Applications (Real Life/Industrial)

- **Gaming PCs:** ATX motherboards **provide high-performance expandability.**
- **Workstations:** E-ATX motherboards support multiple GPUs and high-speed processing.
- **Embedded Systems:** Mini-ITX motherboards are used in smart appliances and automotive systems.
- **Server Racks:** Rack-mounted motherboards optimize data centre efficiency.

Case Study (Environmental/Sustainability Issues)

- **E-Waste from Outdated Motherboards:** Large-scale disposal contributes to **global electronic waste concerns.**
- **Energy-Efficient Motherboards:** Low-power designs reduce carbon footprint.
- **Recyclable Components:** Some manufacturers design eco-friendly motherboard materials.

Create Inquisitiveness and Curiosity

- Why do different motherboard sizes exist, and how do they impact performance?
- How does motherboard selection affect gaming performance?
- What are the future trends in motherboard design?

Solved Problems (With Increasing Difficulty Level)

1. **Motherboard Power Consumption:** If an ATX motherboard uses 50W and a Mini-ITX motherboard uses 30W, what is the annual energy difference?
2. **Expansion Slot Calculation:** Given a Micro-ATX motherboard with 4 PCIe slots, determine how many expansion cards can be installed.
3. **Motherboard Compatibility Analysis:** If a processor requires an LGA 1700 socket, which motherboard form factors support it?

SUMMARY

- Motherboards come in various form factors, including ATX, Micro-ATX, and Mini-ITX.
- Choosing the right motherboard depends on size, expandability, and power compatibility.
- Modern motherboards integrate advanced technologies, including Wi-Fi, NVMe, and AI optimizations.
- Environmental concerns drive the adoption of energy-efficient motherboards.

EXERCISES

1. Subjective Questions

Category-I (Revised Bloom's Level -1, 2 & 3)

1. Define the role of a motherboard in a computer system.
2. Explain the differences between ATX, Micro-ATX, and Mini-ITX motherboards.
3. Describe the advantages of using an ATX motherboard over smaller form factors.

Category-II (Revised Bloom's Level -4, 5 & 6)

1. Compare the suitability of Mini-ITX motherboards for gaming vs. workstation PCs.
2. Discuss the impact of AI integration in modern motherboard designs.

2.2 MOTHERBOARD COMPONENTS AND EXPANSION SLOTS

The motherboard serves as the backbone of a computer system, connecting various components and allowing communication between them. It includes several essential **components and expansion slots**, each with a distinct role in ensuring the system's functionality and scalability.

Active vs. Passive Motherboards

Motherboards can be classified into **active** and **passive** designs based on the presence of processing capability and additional components.

- **Active Motherboards:** Feature built-in controllers, chipsets, and voltage regulators to handle processing tasks efficiently.
- **Passive Motherboards:** Rely on external processing cards or modules for operation, often used in legacy and industrial computing environments.

Key Components of a Motherboard

1. **Chipsets:** Control communication between the CPU, memory, storage, and peripherals. Modern motherboards include two primary chipsets:
   - **Northbridge:** Handles high-speed communication between the CPU, RAM, and graphics card.
   - **Southbridge:** Manages slower connections like USB, SATA, and network interfaces.
2. **CPU Socket:** The slot where the processor is installed. Common types include:
   - **LGA (Land Grid Array):** Used by Intel processors, with contact pins on the motherboard.
   - **PGA (Pin Grid Array):** Used by AMD processors, with pins on the CPU itself.
   - **BGA (Ball Grid Array):** Permanently soldered CPUs common in embedded systems.
3. **Memory Slots (DIMM Slots):** Provide installation points for RAM modules. Most modern motherboards support DDR4 and DDR5 RAM, with dual-channel or quad-channel memory configurations.
4. **Expansion Slots:** Enable the addition of graphics cards, network adapters, and storage controllers. Common types include:
   - **PCIe (Peripheral Component Interconnect Express):** Standard high-speed interface for modern expansion cards.
   - **PCI:** Older expansion slot format, still used in some legacy systems.
   - **AGP (Accelerated Graphics Port):** Previously used for dedicated graphics cards, it is now obsolete.

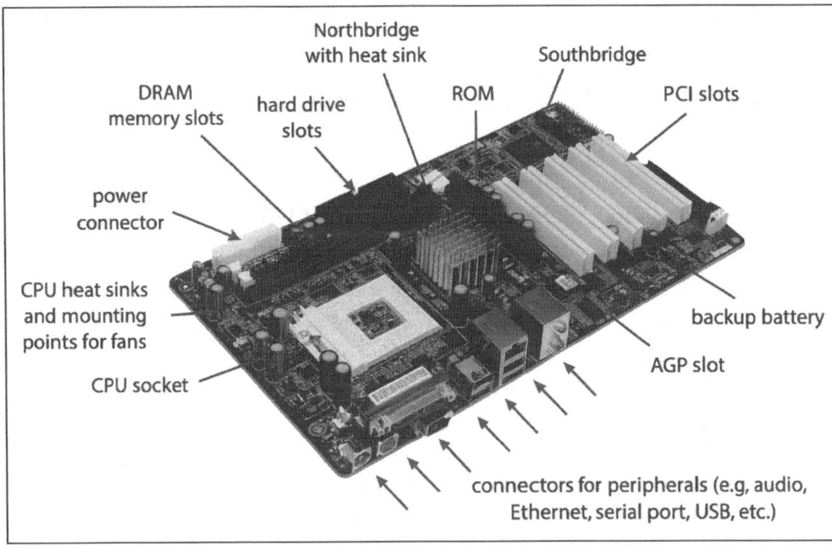

Figure 2.2: *Motherboard Layout Showing Key Components*

Figure 2.2 illustrates the Motherboard Layout, showcasing key components essential for computer functionality. The CPU socket serves as the central processing unit's mounting point, with adjacent heat sinks and fan mounting points for cooling. DRAM memory slots allow for RAM installation, providing high-speed data access to the processor. The Northbridge and Southbridge chipsets manage communication between the CPU, RAM, and peripheral components.

The motherboard also features PCI and AGP slots for expansion cards, such as graphics and sound cards, while complicated drive slots accommodate storage devices. A power connector supplies the necessary voltage to the system, and a backup battery maintains BIOS settings. Additionally, connectors for USB, Ethernet, and audio peripherals enable external device integration. The motherboard's architecture ensures efficient communication between components, optimizing computing performance and expandability.

M.2 and DIMM.2 Expansion Slots

Modern motherboards incorporate M.2 and DIMM.2 slots for high-speed storage and expansion.

- **M.2 Slot:** Supports NVMe SSDs for ultra-fast storage performance.
- **DIMM.2 Slot:** Allows additional expansion for SSDs using a RAM-like form factor.

Intel D850GB and Motherboard Compatibility

The **Intel D850GB motherboard** was a pivotal design featuring RAMBUS memory support, setting a foundation for future high-performance motherboards. Compatibility factors include:

- **Chipset support:** Determines the type of processors and memory that can be used.
- **BIOS/UEFI firmware:** Ensures hardware compatibility and security.

- **RGB Headers and Customization:** Enables LED lighting control for aesthetics and system monitoring.

Power Connectors and Voltage Regulation

Motherboards require stable power delivery to function correctly. Common power connectors include:

- **24-Pin ATX Power Connector:** Supplies power to the entire motherboard.
- **8-Pin CPU Power Connector:** Dedicated power for high-performance processors.
- **SATA and PCIe Power Connectors:** Provide power to storage devices and graphics cards.

Modern motherboards integrate voltage regulation modules (VRMs) to maintain a stable power supply, especially during overclocking and high-load operations.

BIOS and UEFI Firmware

The Basic Input/Output System (BIOS) and Unified Extensible Firmware Interface (UEFI) provide low-level hardware initialization and configuration.

- **BIOS:** Legacy firmware controlling boot processes and hardware interaction.
- **UEFI:** Modern replacement with a graphical interface, enhanced security, and faster boot times.

Conclusion

Motherboards house critical components that determine a computer's performance and expansion capabilities. With advancements in chipsets, expansion slots, power management, and firmware technologies, modern motherboards offer improved efficiency and reliability for diverse computing applications.

The following section explores motherboard connectivity and upgrading options, detailing compatibility considerations and expansion capabilities.

Interesting Facts

- **Central Role:** The motherboard acts as the central nervous system of a computer, linking all components together for seamless communication.
- **Historical Milestone:** Early computers featured rudimentary boards, whereas today's motherboards integrate sophisticated controllers and power management systems.
- **Customization Culture:** From overclocking to RGB lighting, modern users modify motherboards to both boost performance and enhance aesthetics.

Video Resources

- **Overview of Motherboards:** Videos explaining the layout and purpose of motherboard components are plentiful. Recommended search terms include "Motherboard Fundamentals" and "How Motherboards Work."
- **Exploring Expansion Slots:** Tutorials detailing the evolution and differences between PCI, AGP, and PCIe slots are ideal for visual learners.
- **Hands-On Guides:** Look for assembly videos that cover BIOS/UEFI configuration, troubleshooting common issues, and component installation.

Tip: YouTube channels such as *Linus Tech Tips* and *Techquickie* often provide in-depth, easy-to-follow guides.

Use of ICT in Motherboard Technology

- **System Integration:** ICT relies on motherboards to integrate processing, storage, and connectivity, forming the backbone of modern digital systems.
- **Connectivity for Communication:** With built-in interfaces for networking and peripheral devices, motherboards enable efficient data exchange essential for both personal and industrial ICT applications.
- **Smart Devices and IoT:** Specialized motherboards power a range of IoT devices and embedded systems, ensuring reliable real-time performance.

Applications (Real Life / Industrial)

- **Everyday Computing:** Desktops, laptops, and workstations all depend on motherboards, making them indispensable for daily tasks.
- **Data Centers and High-Performance Servers:** Advanced motherboards with multiple expansion slots support complex tasks and high-speed data processing in enterprise environments.
- **Industrial Automation:** In manufacturing and automation, rugged motherboards power systems that control robotics, sensors, and other machinery.
- **Embedded and IoT Systems:** From automotive control systems to smart home devices, specialized motherboards ensure stability and efficiency even in challenging environments.

Case Study: Environmental Sustainability and Ethical Issues

Context

The production and disposal of electronic components contribute to significant environmental challenges, including e-waste and the use of hazardous materials.

Scenario

A tech company implements a new design for their motherboards by:

- Adopting lead-free solder and using eco-friendly materials.
- Designing modular motherboards that can be easily repaired or upgraded, extending product life.
- Launching recycling programs to reclaim valuable components and reduce waste.

Discussion Points

- **Environmental Impact:** How do sustainable manufacturing practices help minimize e-waste?
- **Corporate Ethics:** What ethical responsibilities do companies have in reducing their ecological footprint?
- **Design Innovation:** In what ways can engineering innovations lead to greener, more efficient electronic devices?

Creating Inquisitiveness and Curiosity

Stimulate deeper thinking with questions such as:

- **Comparative Inquiry:** What are the benefits and potential limitations of active versus passive motherboard designs in various environments?
- **Future Prospects:** How might emerging trends like AI, machine learning, or edge computing influence the design of future motherboards?
- **Sustainability Challenge:** What innovative design changes could further reduce the environmental impact of electronic waste?

Solved Problems (With Increasing Difficulty Level)

Problem 1 (Basic)

Question

Define the main difference between active and passive motherboards.

Solution

Active motherboards integrate essential components like chipsets, controllers, and voltage regulators for processing tasks. In contrast, passive motherboards rely on external modules or cards, a design more common in legacy or specialized industrial systems.

Problem 2 (Intermediate)

Question

Describe the functions of the northbridge and southbridge on a motherboard.

Solution

- **North bridge:** Facilitates high-speed communication between the CPU, RAM, and graphics cards.
- **South bridge:** Manages slower connections, such as those for USB ports, SATA devices, and network interfaces.

Problem 3 (Advanced)

Question

In a scenario requiring high durability and reliability under harsh conditions, which motherboard type (active or passive) might be preferred, and why?

Solution

A passive motherboard may be favoured because it allows for the use of external processing modules that can be replaced or upgraded independently, enhancing overall system durability and easing maintenance in challenging environments.

Problem 4 (Challenging)

Question

Explain the evolution from AGP to PCIe expansion slots and discuss how this transition has impacted system performance and future scalability.

Solution

- **Enhanced Bandwidth:** PCIe offers multiple data lanes, significantly increasing transfer rates compared to the older AGP standard.
- **Modularity and Flexibility:** PCIe slots allow for the addition of a range of high-performance components, including advanced graphics cards and network adapters.
- **Future-Proofing:** The scalable nature of PCIe ensures compatibility with emerging technologies, thereby extending system longevity and performance.

2.3 MOTHERBOARD CONNECTIVITY AND UPGRADING MOTHERBOARDS

Motherboard Connectivity Overview

A motherboard acts as a hub for data transmission between various components of a computer system. Efficient connectivity options ensure seamless communication between the CPU, memory, storage, peripherals, and external devices. Modern motherboards incorporate a variety of ports, sockets, and expansion slots to accommodate evolving hardware standards.

Next-Gen Connectivity Features

To enhance performance and usability, contemporary motherboards integrate high-speed connectivity technologies such as:

- **USB 3.1 Gen2:** Delivers up to 10Gbps transfer speeds, twice as fast as USB 3.0.
- **Thunderbolt 4:** Supports 40Gbps data transmission, enabling high-speed external device connections.
- **Wi-Fi 6 and 802.11 AD:** Advanced wireless networking for faster and more stable internet connections.
- **PCIe Gen4 & Gen5:** Provides double the bandwidth of PCIe Gen3, improving GPU and SSD performance.

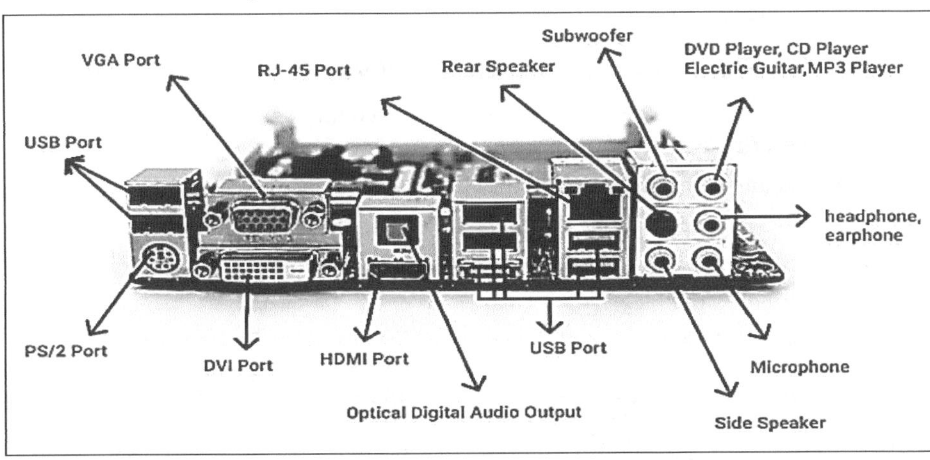

Figure 2.3: Motherboard Connectivity Ports and Expansion Slots

Figure 2.3 illustrates the Motherboard Connectivity Ports and Expansion Slots, highlighting various input and output interfaces used for peripheral connections. The VGA, DVI, and HDMI ports allow for video output to monitors, supporting different display technologies. The RJ-45 port provides Ethernet connectivity for wired networking, while multiple USB ports enable connections for external devices such as keyboards, mice, and storage drives.

For audio output, the motherboard features dedicated ports for rear speakers, subwoofers, side speakers, and headphones, supporting surround sound systems. The microphone input facilitates voice recording and communication, while the optical digital audio output ensures high-quality audio transmission. Additionally, the PS/2 port is included for legacy keyboard and mouse connections, and the expansion slots accommodate various multimedia and gaming peripherals. These connectivity options enhance the motherboard's versatility, allowing seamless integration with multiple devices for an optimized computing experience.

Upgrading a Motherboard: Key Considerations

Upgrading a motherboard requires careful assessment of compatibility, expansion needs, and future-proofing factors. The following aspects should be evaluated before upgrading:

1. Processor and Chipset Compatibility

Each motherboard supports a specific set of CPU models and chipsets. Verifying the socket type (e.g., LGA1700 for Intel, AM5 for AM(d) ensures compatibility with modern processors.

2. Memory and Storage Support

Motherboards have designated DIMM slots for RAM modules. It is crucial to ensure:

- **Supported RAM type:** DDR3, DDR4, or DDR5.
- **Maximum memory capacity:** High-end motherboards support 128GB or more.
- **Dual-Channel or Quad-Channel Support:** Optimizes data transfer efficiency.
- **NVMe and SATA SSD Support:** M.2 slots offer faster storage speeds compared to traditional SATA ports.

3. Expansion Slots and Graphics Card Support

Modern motherboards feature multiple PCIe slots to accommodate graphics cards, network adapters, and sound cards. Key factors include:

- **PCIe Lane Allocation:** Determines GPU performance efficiency.
- **Multi-GPU Support:** Enables CrossFire (AM(d) or SLI (NVIDI(a) configurations.
- **USB and PCIe Power Considerations:** Ensures stable power delivery for high-performance peripherals.

Table 2.2: *Comparison of PCIe Gen3, Gen4, and Gen5 Performance*

Feature	PCIe Gen3	PCIe Gen4	PCIe Gen5
Bandwidth per lane	8 GT/s	16 GT/s	32 GT/s
Total Bandwidth (x16)	128 GB/s	256 GB/s	512 GB/s

Feature	PCIe Gen3	PCIe Gen4	PCIe Gen5
Latency	Moderate	Low	Very Low
Power Efficiency	Standard	Improved	Highly Optimized
Use Cases	Gaming, Work-stations	High-Speed NVMe, AI Applications	Data Centers, HPC, Ad-vanced AI

Table 2.2 compares PCIe Gen3, Gen4, and Gen5 performance, focusing on bandwidth, latency, power efficiency, and use cases. PCIe Gen5 offers the highest bandwidth and lowest latency, making it ideal for data centres and high-performance computing (HP(c). At the same time, Gen4 is optimized for NVMe storage and AI applications, and Gen3 remains suitable for gaming and workstation use.

DDR4 BOOST and Memory Optimization

The **DDR4 BOOST** technology improves RAM performance by reducing latency and increasing bandwidth. Features include:

- **Optimized PCB Layout:** Prevents signal interference for stable overclocking.
- **XMP (Extreme Memory Profile) Support:** Allows memory modules to operate at maximum rated speeds.
- **Error-Correction Code (EC(c) Memory:** Ensures data integrity for workstation-grade applications.

Live Dash OLED Integration and Smart Diagnostics

High-end motherboards now feature Live Dash OLED displays that provide real-time system diagnostics, CPU temperatures, and clock speeds. These displays assist users in:

- **Monitoring hardware performance** without external software.
- **Detecting hardware failures** during system startup.
- **Customizing user interfaces** for system personalization.

Conclusion

Upgrading a motherboard can significantly enhance system performance, connectivity, and future compatibility. With the adoption of next-gen interfaces, advanced memory optimization, and smart monitoring technologies, modern motherboards offer improved efficiency and scalability.

The following section will explore BIOS/UEFI firmware, security enhancements, and motherboard troubleshooting techniques.

Interesting Facts

- **Hub of Communication:** Modern motherboards are not only responsible for connecting internal components but also serve as gateways to high-speed external data transfers, bridging devices from USB drives to next-gen wireless networks.
- **Evolution in Connectivity:** With each generation—from USB 2.0 to USB 3.1 Gen2, and from PCIe Gen3 to Gen5—the speed and efficiency of data transfer have doubled or more, dramatically changing computing performance.

- **Smart Integration:** High-end motherboards now integrate real-time diagnostic displays (like Live Dash OLEDs), allowing users to monitor system health directly on the board.

Video Resources

- **Overview Videos:** Look for videos on "Motherboard Connectivity Explained" or "How to Upgrade Your Motherboard" on platforms like YouTube.
- **In-Depth Tutorials:** Channels such as *Linus Tech Tips* and *Techquickie* offer clear, practical guides on the specifics of USB 3.1, Thunderbolt 4, and PCIe upgrades.
- **Tech Reviews:** Reviews that compare different motherboard models can provide insights into connectivity options and upgrade benefits.

Use of ICT

- **Integrated Communication:** ICT relies on robust and reliable connectivity. Motherboards embody this by connecting CPUs, memory, and peripherals, facilitating high-speed data exchange.
- **Network Capabilities:** With built-in Wi-Fi 6 and advanced LAN options, motherboards support critical ICT infrastructure in smart homes, offices, and industries.
- **Remote Management:** Modern boards offer features like remote diagnostics and firmware updates (BIOS/UEFI), which are key for maintaining ICT systems across distributed networks.

Applications (Real Life/Industrial)

- **Personal Computing:** Upgrading connectivity can enhance gaming experiences, multimedia editing, and everyday productivity by ensuring smooth data flow.
- **Data Centers & Enterprise:** High-performance connectivity options (like PCIe Gen5 and Thunderbolt 4) are crucial for servers and workstations that manage massive datasets and require ultra-low latency.
- **Industrial Automation:** In manufacturing and robotics, reliable high-speed data transfer supports real-time monitoring and control systems, ensuring operational efficiency and safety.
- **Smart Environments:** In IoT applications, advanced connectivity on motherboards helps link sensors and devices, powering smart cities and intelligent infrastructure.

Case Study: Environmental/Sustainability/Social/Ethical Issues

Context

Electronic waste is a growing environmental concern. Upgrading and replacing motherboards contribute significantly to e-waste unless sustainable practices are employed.

Scenario

A leading tech manufacturer implemented an upgrade strategy focused on sustainability by:

- **Modular Design:** Creating motherboards with easily replaceable components to extend the life of the system rather than replacing the entire board.

- **Eco-friendly Materials:** Using recyclable materials and lead-free solder to reduce toxic waste.
- **Recycling Programs:** Collaborating with e-waste recyclers to recover valuable metals and reduce landfill contributions.

Discussion Points

- **Environmental Impact:** How do modular designs and eco-friendly materials lower the carbon footprint of technology upgrades?
- **Corporate Ethics:** What ethical responsibilities do companies have in mitigating e-waste and promoting sustainable practices?
- **Social Considerations:** How can the industry balance rapid technological advancement with long-term environmental stewardship?

Creating Inquisitiveness and Curiosity

- **Open-Ended Questions:**
  - How might the integration of next-gen connectivity (e.g., PCIe Gen5) transform not only gaming but also applications like AI and big data analytics?
  - What are the potential challenges in adopting sustainable practices in high-performance computing environments?
  - Can we think of innovative ways to further enhance motherboard connectivity beyond current technologies?
- **Challenge Learners:** Encourage exploring the interplay between hardware upgrades and overall system performance, and consider how future connectivity standards could revolutionize ICT.

Solved Problems (With Increasing Difficulty Level)

Problem 1 (Basic)

Question

What is the main advantage of USB 3.1 Gen2 over USB 3.0?

Solution

USB 3.1 Gen2 delivers speeds up to 10Gbps, which is twice as fast as USB 3.0, allowing for quicker data transfers and improved peripheral performance.

Problem 2 (Intermediate)

Question

Explain why PCIe Gen4 and Gen5 are important for modern graphics cards and SSDs.

Solution

PCIe Gen4 and Gen5 provide significantly higher bandwidth than previous generations doubling with each generation). This higher data throughput is essential for the faster, more demanding data requirements of modern graphics cards and NVMe SSDs, ensuring smoother performance and reduced bottlenecks.

Problem 3 (Advanced)

Question

How does the choice of motherboard connectivity affect the upgrade path for a high-performance workstation intended for AI applications?

Solution

A motherboard with advanced connectivity options such as PCIe Gen5, Thunderbolt 4, and high-speed LAN is crucial for AI applications. These features ensure that data flows quickly between the CPU, GPUs, and storage devices, which is vital for processing large datasets and complex computations. Additionally, such connectivity provides future-proofing for upgrades, allowing the workstation to adapt to emerging AI hardware advancements.

Problem 4 (Challenging)

Question

Discuss the potential environmental benefits and challenges of implementing a modular motherboard design in terms of sustainability.

Solution

Benefits

- **Extended Lifespan:** Modular designs allow individual components to be upgraded without replacing the entire motherboard, reducing waste.
- **Resource Efficiency:** Fewer resources are used when only specific modules are replaced.

Challenges

- **Design Complexity:** Creating a modular design that maintains performance and reliability can be technically challenging.
- **Cost:** Modular components might be more expensive to produce, potentially affecting overall market adoption.

2.4 BIOS, UEFI FIRMWARE, AND TROUBLESHOOTING

Introduction to BIOS and UEFI

The Basic Input/Output System (BIOS) and Unified Extensible Firmware Interface (UEFI) are fundamental firmware interfaces that initialize hardware components and facilitate the boot process before an operating system loads. BIOS was the standard for decades, but UEFI has replaced it in modern systems due to its enhanced capabilities, security features, and user-friendly graphical interface.

BIOS: Legacy Firmware

BIOS is a low-level firmware stored in a computer's ROM (Read-Only Memory) or Flash Memory. It performs hardware initialization, power-on self-test (POST), and bootstrapping to load the OS.

Key Features of BIOS

- Operates in 16-bit real mode with limited memory access.
- Uses Master Boot Record (MBR) to locate the OS bootloader.
- Limited support for high-capacity storage devices beyond 2TB.
- Accessed via a keyboard-controlled text-based interface.

Figure 2.4 illustrates the BIOS Boot Process, outlining the sequence of steps that occur when a computer starts up. The process begins with the BIOS (Basic Input/Output System), which is responsible for initializing the hardware and performing system checks. Once complete, the BIOS retrieves boot instructions from the Master Boot Record (MBR) located at the start of the primary storage disk.

The MBR then identifies the active partition, which contains the necessary boot files, and loads the boot sector from this partition. Finally, the bootloader executes, loading the operating system's kernel from its filesystem. This structured boot sequence ensures a smooth transition from hardware initialization to operating system execution, allowing the computer to become fully operational.

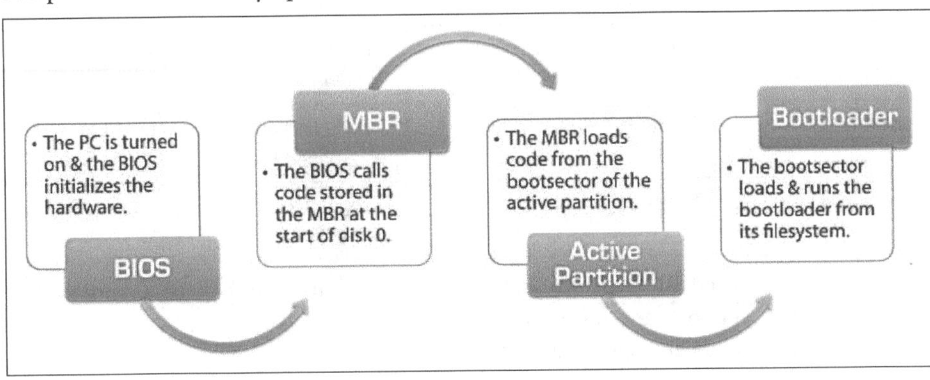

Figure 2.4: *BIOS Boot Process*

UEFI: The Modern Replacement

UEFI is an advanced replacement for BIOS, offering a more robust, secure, and faster booting environment. It is stored in EEPROM (Electrically Erasable Programmable Read-Only Memory) or on dedicated Flash Memory.

Key Features of UEFI

- Supports 32-bit and 64-bit processing, enabling a graphical interface.
- It uses the GUID Partition Table (GPT), allowing support for hard drives larger than 2TB.
- It provides a secure boot, preventing unauthorized bootloaders and malware execution.
- Supports mouse navigation and network-based firmware updates.

Table 2.3 compares BIOS and UEFI, highlighting their differences in boot mode, user interface, partitioning, security, and compatibility. UEFI provides faster boot times, enhanced security with Secure Boot, support for more extensive storage drives, and modern networking features.

In contrast, BIOS remains simpler but is limited in capabilities and legacy hardware support.

Table 2.3: *Comparison of BIOS and UEFI*

Feature	BIOS (Legacy)	UEFI (Modern)
Boot Mode	16-bit real mode	32-bit or 64-bit mode
User Interface	Text-based, keyboard-only	Graphical UI supports mouse navigation
Partitioning Scheme	MBR (Master Boot Recor(d)	GPT (GUID Partition Table)
Max Drive Support	Up to 2TB	Over 9ZB (Zettabytes)
Security	Minimal, no Secure Boot	Secure Boot prevents unauthorized software execution
Speed	Slower boot times	Faster boot times with optimized initialization
Firmware Storage	ROM or Flash Memory	EEPROM or Flash Memory
Networking	Limited (PXE Boot Support)	Full networking stack for remote updates and diagnostics
Updates	Requires manual updating	Can be updated via the internet (network-based firmware updates)
Compatibility	Supports older hardware	Designed for modern systems, backwards compatible with BIOS

UEFI has replaced BIOS in modern computers due to its enhanced security, more extensive storage support, and faster booting capabilities. However, legacy BIOS remains relevant for older hardware systems and industrial applications.

Accessing BIOS/UEFI Settings

Users can enter BIOS/UEFI settings by pressing a designated key (e.g., F2, DEL, or ES(c) during system startup.

Within these settings, users can:

- Configure boot priority (e.g., HDD, SSD, USB, Network Boot).
- Adjust CPU, RAM, and voltage settings for overclocking.
- Turn hardware virtualization on or off.
- Update firmware through BIOS/UEFI Flash Utility.

Motherboard Troubleshooting Techniques

Motherboard issues can result in system instability, boot failures, or hardware malfunctions. Troubleshooting methods help diagnose and resolve common problems effectively.

1. Power-On Self-Test (POST) Errors

When a motherboard fails to initialize properly, it generates POST beep codes or LED error indicators. These codes indicate issues with the CPU, RAM, or GPU.

Common POST Error Beep Codes:

- **Beep:** Successful boot.
- **Short Beeps:** Minor error, the system continues booting.
- **Beeps:** CPU failure.
- **Continuous Beeping:** RAM or GPU issue.

2. No Power or Boot Failure

If the system does not power on, follow these steps:

- Verify the 24-pin ATX and 8-pin CPU power connections.
- Reset the CMOS battery to clear incorrect BIOS settings.
- Check the power supply unit (PSU) using a tester.

3. Overheating Issues

- Ensure thermal paste is applied between the CPU and heat sink.
- Check for proper airflow and functioning fans.
- Monitor temperatures using UEFI diagnostics tools.

4. Peripheral Device Failures

- Ensure PCIe expansion cards (e.g., GPUs, Wi-Fi cards) are properly seated.
- Update BIOS/UEFI firmware to fix compatibility issues.
- Reinstall device drivers in the operating system.

Updating BIOS/UEFI Firmware

Manufacturers release BIOS/UEFI updates to improve hardware support and fix security vulnerabilities. The update process involves:

1. Downloading the latest firmware from the manufacturer's website.
2. Loading the **update onto a USB drive formatted in FAT32.**
3. **Using the BIOS Flash Utility to apply the update.**

Figure 2.4 illustrates the BIOS Update Process, outlining the sequential steps involved in updating a system's BIOS/UEFI firmware. The process begins with downloading the latest firmware from the manufacturer's official website to ensure compatibility with the motherboard. The firmware is then copied onto a USB drive formatted in FAT32, preparing it for installation.

Next, the system is restarted, and the user enters the BIOS interface, where the BIOS Flash Utility is accessed. The update file is selected from the USB drive, and the update process is initiated. If the update is successful, the system restarts automatically, applying the changes.

However, in case of failure, the user may need to retry the process to ensure that the correct firmware file is used. This update process is crucial for improving hardware compatibility, system stability, and security by addressing firmware vulnerabilities.

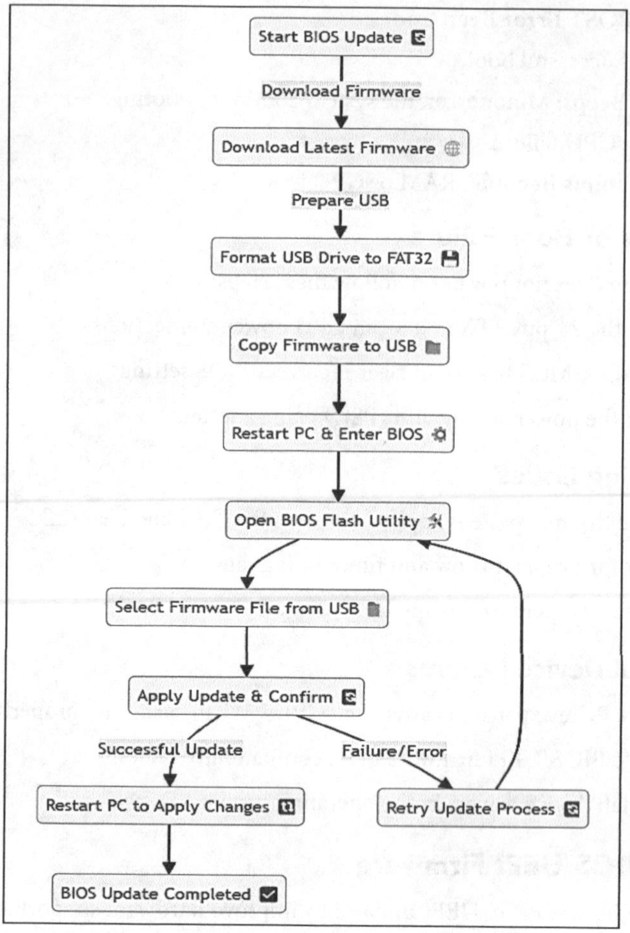

***Figure 2.4:** BIOS Update Process*

Conclusion

BIOS and UEFI play a crucial role in system initialization and hardware management. While BIOS remains relevant for older systems, UEFI provides superior performance, security, and scalability for modern computers. Understanding motherboard troubleshooting techniques ensures efficient system maintenance and reliability.

Interesting Facts

- **Foundational Role:** BIOS and UEFI are the first pieces of software that run when a computer is powered on, kickstarting the hardware and loading the operating system.
- **Evolution Over Time:** While BIOS was the standard for decades, UEFI now leads modern systems with faster boot times, a graphical interface, and advanced security features.
- **Security Enhancement:** UEFI's Secure Boot feature helps protect our computer from malware and unauthorized bootloaders—a significant leap in system security.

Video Resources

- **Introductory Overviews:** Search YouTube for "BIOS vs UEFI Explained" to find clear, animated tutorials that break down their differences and functions.
- **Step-by-Step Guides:** Videos titled "How to Update Your BIOS/UEFI" or "Troubleshooting POST Errors" can provide practical, visual guidance for hands-on learners.
- **Expert Discussions:** Look for tech review videos that discuss firmware evolution, such as those by *Linus Tech Tips* or *Techquickie*, which often highlight the impact of UEFI on modern computing.

Use of ICT

- **System Initialization:** Both BIOS and UEFI play a critical role in ICT by initializing and configuring hardware components before the operating system takes control, ensuring seamless operation across diverse computing environments.
- **Network Diagnostics:** Modern UEFI firmware includes network-based tools for remote updates and diagnostics, which are crucial for managing enterprise and IoT networks efficiently.
- **Data Security:** With Secure Boot and other security features, UEFI supports the integrity of ICT systems by blocking unauthorized software during startup.

Applications (Real Life/Industrial)

- **Personal Computers:** Almost every desktop or laptop relies on BIOS/UEFI to properly initialize the hardware, making these firmware interfaces essential for daily computing tasks.
- **Enterprise Environments:** Data centres and corporate IT setups use UEFI's advanced features (like remote firmware updates and secure boot) to maintain system reliability and security.
- **Industrial Systems:** Legacy systems may still use BIOS for stability and compatibility in environments where older hardware is prevalent, while newer industrial applications benefit from UEFI's scalability and enhanced diagnostics.

Case Study: Environmental/Sustainability/Social/Ethical Issues

Context

Firmware updates and system maintenance can impact not only system performance but also environmental sustainability by extending hardware life and reducing e-waste.

Scenario

An IT company adopted a regular firmware update policy for its fleet of computers to ensure optimal performance and security. They also promoted UEFI's features to support longer hardware lifespans, reducing the frequency of complete system replacements.

- **Sustainability Impact:** Regular updates help maintain the relevance of older hardware, thereby lowering e-waste.
- **Ethical Considerations:** Companies are encouraged to manage hardware upgrades and disposal responsibly, contributing to broader corporate social responsibility initiatives.

- **Discussion Points:**
  - How can firmware updates be leveraged to extend the life of electronic devices?
  - What responsibilities do manufacturers have in ensuring the sustainability of their products?

Creating Inquisitiveness and Curiosity

Open-Ended Questions:

- What might be the future developments in firmware technology beyond UEFI?
- How does Secure Boot contribute to overall cybersecurity strategies in enterprise environments?
- In what ways can firmware troubleshooting techniques be improved with emerging diagnostic technologies?

Hands-On Exploration:

- Encourage learners to access their own computer's BIOS/UEFI settings and explore options such as boot priority, hardware diagnostics, and overclocking settings to see these concepts in action.

Solved Problems (With Increasing Difficulty L3evel)

Problem 1 (Basic)

Question

What is the primary function of BIOS in a computer system?

Solution

BIOS is responsible for performing the Power-On Self-Test (POST), initializing hardware components, and loading the operating system's bootloader.

Problem 2 (Intermediate)

Question

How does UEFI improve upon traditional BIOS in terms of storage support?

Solution

UEFI uses the GUID Partition Table (GPT), which supports hard drives larger than 2TB—far exceeding the 2TB limit of the MBR partitioning scheme used by BIOS.

Problem 3 (Advanced)

Question

Explain how Secure Boot in UEFI enhances system security.

Solution

Secure Boot ensures that only authorized bootloaders and trusted operating system components are executed during startup, which helps prevent malware or unauthorized code from taking control of the system.

Problem 4 (Challenging)

Question

Discuss a troubleshooting scenario where a computer fails to boot and describe the steps we would take using BIOS/UEFI tools to diagnose the problem.

Solution

- **Observe POST Codes:** Listen for beep codes or view LED error indicators to identify hardware issues (e.g., RAM or GPU problems).
- **Check BIOS/UEFI Settings:**
  - Verify boot priority settings to ensure the correct drive is selected.
  - Reset the CMOS battery if there are configuration errors.
- **Update Firmware:**
  - If hardware seems functional but issues persist, update the BIOS/UEFI firmware to fix known bugs or compatibility issues.
- **Monitor Hardware:**
  - Use built-in UEFI diagnostics to check CPU temperatures, voltage regulation, and system logs for signs of overheating or power issues.

2.5 COMMON MOTHERBOARD ISSUES AND TROUBLESHOOTING TECHNIQUES

Motherboard failures can cause system instability, boot errors, and hardware malfunctions. Understanding common issues and applying effective troubleshooting techniques can help diagnose and resolve problems efficiently.

Power Issues

A computer failing to power on is often linked to motherboard-related power issues. Common causes and solutions include:

- **Faulty Power Supply Unit (PSU):** Test using a PSU tester or replace the unit.
- **Loose Power Cables:** Ensure the 24-pin ATX and 8-pin CPU power connectors are firmly seated.
- **Short Circuits:** Remove non-essential components and check for motherboard shorts using an insulation mat.
- **CMOS Battery Failure:** Replace the CR2032 CMOS battery if the system does not retain BIOS settings.

Boot and POST Errors

During startup, a motherboard performs a Power-On Self-Test (POST) to verify hardware integrity. If errors occur, troubleshooting involves:

- **Beep Code Analysis:** Check motherboard documentation for POST beep code interpretations.
- **No Display Issues:** Reseat the GPU and RAM, ensuring correct placement.
- **BIOS Corruption:** Recover using BIOS flashback or resetting to factory defaults.

Overheating Problems

Overheating can cause system crashes, slow performance, and even permanent hardware damage. Preventive measures include:

- **Verifying CPU Cooler Installation:** Ensure the heatsink and thermal paste are properly applied.
- **Improving Airflow:** Install additional case fans or reposition components for better ventilation.
- **Cleaning Dust Buildup:** Regularly clean heat sinks, fans, and vents using compressed air.
- **Monitoring Temperatures:** Use BIOS or software tools like HWMonitor to track heat levels.

Peripheral and Expansion Slot Failures

If connected devices (USB, PCIe cards, or storage drives) are not functioning correctly:

- **Inspect Expansion Slots:** Reseat PCIe and RAM modules, ensuring proper connection.
- **Update Drivers:** Ensure all chipset and device drivers are up to date.
- **Test on Another System:** Confirm the peripheral works on a different PC to rule out hardware failure.

BIOS/UEFI Update Failures

Updating the BIOS/UEFI can resolve compatibility issues but may introduce new problems if improperly executed. To avoid failures:

- **Use Manufacturer-Approved Firmware:** Download updates from the motherboard vendor's official website.
- **Ensure Uninterrupted Power Supply:** Avoid BIOS corruption by preventing power loss during updates.
- **Backup BIOS Settings:** Save current configurations before flashing new firmware.

Table 2.4: *Troubleshooting Motherboard-Specific Errors*

Issue	Possible Cause	Solution
No Power	Faulty PSU or loose cable	Replace PSU, reconnect cables
No Display	GPU or RAM issues	Reseat components, test with one RAM stick
Frequent Crashes	Overheating or power instability	Check cooling, replace PSU
USB/PCIe Failures	Driver or hardware malfunction	Update drivers, test in another slot

Table 2.4 outlines common motherboard-specific errors, their possible causes, and recommended troubleshooting solutions. Issues such as no power, no display, frequent crashes, and USB/PCIe failures can often be resolved by checking hardware connections, updating drivers, improving cooling, or replacing faulty components.

Conclusion

Motherboard troubleshooting involves a systematic approach to diagnosing hardware failures. By identifying power issues, POST errors, overheating, peripheral failures, and BIOS update errors, users can apply practical solutions to maintain system stability and performance.

The following section will focus on case studies of motherboard failures and best practices for long-term system maintenance.

1. Interesting Facts

- **Frequent Culprit:** Motherboard issues are often at the heart of many system failures, as they directly affect multiple components and overall performance.
- **Diagnostic Clues:** POST beep codes and LED error indicators are invaluable clues that help pinpoint specific hardware issues.
- **Preventive Maintenance:** Regular cleaning, proper cable management, and firmware backups can significantly reduce the occurrence of motherboard-related problems.

2. Video Resources

- **Troubleshooting Tutorials:** Search for "Motherboard Troubleshooting" or "Diagnosing POST Errors" on YouTube for practical, step-by-step guidance.
- **Maintenance Guides:** Videos demonstrating cleaning techniques and proper installation of components (like CPU coolers and power cables) can be beneficial.
- **Expert Interviews:** Tech channels such as *Linus Tech Tips* often discuss common issues and innovative repair techniques.

3. Use of ICT in Troubleshooting

- **Diagnostic Software:** Programs like HWMonitor and BIOS diagnostics tools help track system temperatures and voltages in real-time, enabling proactive maintenance.
- **Remote Management:** In enterprise environments, network-based tools integrated into modern UEFI firmware allow remote monitoring and firmware updates to prevent failures.
- **Data Logging:** ICT tools that log POST errors and system events can aid in the early detection of recurring issues.

4. Applications (Real Life/Industrial)

- **Personal Systems:** Hobbyists and gamers often encounter issues like overheating and no-display errors, which can be remedied with proper troubleshooting.
- **Workstations and Servers:** In data centres, a single motherboard failure can affect critical operations; hence, robust diagnostics and redundancy planning are vital.
- **Industrial Equipment:** Machines and embedded systems rely on stable motherboards; troubleshooting methods must be adapted for environments with unique operating conditions.

5. Case Study: Environmental/Sustainability / Social/Ethical Issues

Context

Effective troubleshooting and maintenance not only improve system reliability but also extend the life of hardware, reducing electronic waste.

Scenario

A manufacturing firm implemented a regular diagnostic schedule for its computer systems, using automated tools to log and analyze POST errors and temperature spikes. This proactive approach allowed them to replace failing components before complete system breakdowns, extending hardware lifespan and reducing the need for frequent replacements.

Discussion Points

- **Environmental Impact:** Extending hardware life minimizes e-waste and reduces the environmental footprint of IT operations.
- **Ethical Considerations:** Companies have a responsibility to maintain their equipment responsibly, balancing performance needs with sustainable practices.
- **Social Impact:** Reliable systems ensure uninterrupted services in critical applications, benefiting communities that depend on these technologies.

6. Creating Inquisitiveness and Curiosity

- **Exploratory Questions:**
  - What innovative methods could be developed to streamline the troubleshooting process for motherboard issues further?
  - How might AI-powered diagnostics revolutionize hardware maintenance in the future?
  - In what ways can sustainable design practices reduce common motherboard failures over time?
- **Hands-On Challenges:** Encourage learners to document their own troubleshooting experiences, create flowcharts for diagnosing POST errors, or even build DIY diagnostic tools using microcontrollers.

7. Solved Problems (With Increasing Difficulty Level)

Problem 1 (Basic)

Question

What should we check if our computer fails to power on?

Solution

- Verify that the 24-pin ATX and 8-pin CPU power connectors are securely connected.
- Test the power supply unit (PSU) using a PSU tester, or consider replacing it if it is faulty.
- Check for CMOS battery failure and replace it if necessary.

Problem 2 (Intermediate)

Question

A computer passes POST but shows no display. What are the possible causes and steps to resolve this issue?

Solution

- **Possible Causes:**
  - Loose or improperly seated GPU or RAM modules.
  - BIOS corruption causes incorrect display settings.
- **Troubleshooting Steps:**
  - Reseat the GPU and RAM, ensuring they are correctly installed.
  - Consult motherboard documentation for any relevant POST beep codes that may indicate the problem.
  - Reset the BIOS to factory defaults if necessary.

Problem 3 (Advanced)

Question

Describe a systematic approach to diagnose frequent system crashes potentially caused by overheating.

Solution

1. **Verify CPU Cooler Installation:**
   - Ensure that the heatsink is properly attached and that thermal paste is correctly applied.
2. **Improve Airflow:**
   - Check that all case fans are operational and consider adding extra fans or repositioning components to optimize airflow.
3. **Clean Dust Buildup:**
   - Regularly clean heat sinks, fans, and vents using compressed air.
4. **Monitor Temperatures:**
   - Use BIOS diagnostics or software tools like HWMonitor to track system temperatures and adjust cooling as needed.

Problem 4 (Challenging)

Question

How would we troubleshoot a BIOS/UEFI update failure, and what preventive measures can be taken to avoid such issues?

Solution

1. **Troubleshooting Steps:**
   - Confirm that we are using manufacturer-approved firmware downloaded from the official website.

- Ensure that the system has an uninterrupted power supply during the update process; using a UPS can help.
- Back up current BIOS settings before initiating the update to allow a quick recovery if something goes wrong.

2. **Preventive Measures:**
   - Regularly check for firmware updates and read the manufacturer's release notes to understand improvements and fixes.
   - Maintain a detailed log of BIOS settings and updates for future troubleshooting.

2.6 CASE STUDIES AND BEST PRACTICES FOR MOTHERBOARD MAINTENANCE (DETAILED ANALYSIS)

2.6.1 Case Study 1: Motherboard Power Failure in a Business Environment

Background

A mid-sized IT firm with over 200 desktop computers faced recurrent motherboard failures, causing severe work disruptions and productivity loss. Employees reported random shutdowns, system failures, and power cycling issues that significantly impacted workflow efficiency.

The IT department conducted a preliminary assessment and found that the failures were not isolated to a single model or brand of motherboard but were affecting systems across multiple hardware vendors.

Diagnosis

A detailed **diagnostic evaluation** identified the following contributing factors:

1. **Unstable Power Supply:** Frequent voltage fluctuations and sudden power outages were causing repeated power surges, damaging motherboard components.
2. **Faulty Capacitors:** Several affected motherboards had bulging or leaking capacitors, indicative of electrical stress or overheating.
3. **Overloaded Power Strips:** Employees were overloading surge protectors with multiple high-power devices, leading to excessive power draw and fluctuating current supply.
4. **Insufficient Cooling Systems:** Improper ventilation and dust accumulation were causing heat buildup, further stressing the motherboard's voltage regulators.

Solution Implemented

The IT team took immediate action to mitigate power-related motherboard failures:

- **Install UPS (Uninterruptible Power Supply) systems** at all workstations to ensure stable power delivery and prevent sudden shutdowns.
- **Replacement of damaged capacitors** with high-quality, durable alternatives to prevent future power failures.
- **Upgrading power supply units (PSUs)** with higher wattage and 80 Plus Gold certification for efficiency and stable voltage delivery.

- **Reorganizing workstation power management** by limiting high-power devices per power strip and introducing regulated surge protectors.
- **Enhancing airflow within office workstations** by implementing scheduled maintenance for cleaning dust buildup from fans, vents, and power connectors.

These measures resulted in a 70% reduction in motherboard-related failures within six months, improving overall system reliability and longevity.

Figure 2.5 illustrates Damaged Capacitors on a Motherboard, highlighting the potential risks of failing electronic components in a computer system. Capacitors play a crucial role in stabilizing voltage and filtering power fluctuations to ensure reliable motherboard operation. Over time, capacitors may degrade due to excessive heat, power surges, or poor manufacturing quality, leading to bulging, leakage, or complete failure.

Figure 2.5: *Damaged Capacitors on a Motherboard*

Damaged capacitors can cause system instability, random shutdowns, boot failures, or performance degradation. Common signs of capacitor failure include frequent crashes, failure to power on, or distorted audio/video output. To prevent further damage, affected capacitors should be replaced by a technician, and proper cooling mechanisms should be maintained to extend motherboard longevity. Regular hardware inspections and using a high-quality power supply can help mitigate such failures.

2.6.2 Case Study 2: Boot Failure Due to BIOS Corruption

Background

A high-performance gaming PC in a professional eSports training centre failed to boot after a failed BIOS update. The system displayed a blank screen with no POST messages, and the motherboard LED debug indicators pointed to firmware corruption.

The system was a custom-built high-end rig featuring an Intel Core i9 processor, 64GB RAM, and an RTX 4090 GPU. The issue arose after an attempt to update the BIOS firmware using an external USB drive, but the update process was interrupted due to a power failure.

Diagnosis

Upon investigation, the following issues were identified:

1. **BIOS Firmware Corruption:** The BIOS update process was incomplete due to **sudden power loss**, rendering the firmware unbootable.

2. **No POST Beeps or Display Output:** The motherboard failed to initialize, indicating firmware corruption at a critical level.
3. **CMOS Battery Failure:** The battery was drained, preventing proper BIOS resets.
4. **No Backup BIOS Enabled:** The system lacked a dual-BIOS feature, which could have allowed automatic recovery from corruption.

Solution Implemented

To recover the system, the following steps were taken:

- **BIOS Flashback Utility:** Used the motherboard's BIOS flashback feature to reinstall factory firmware using a USB drive containing a fresh firmware file.
- **CMOS Reset:** Removed and replaced the CMOS battery, then reset the BIOS settings using the motherboard's jumper pins.
- **Firmware Redundancy:** Configured a secondary backup BIOS chip to prevent future failures.
- **Uninterruptible Power Supply (UPS):** Ensured future BIOS updates were conducted with a UPS connection to avoid power failures during the flashing process.

After the firmware was successfully restored, the system booted normally, and no further BIOS corruption incidents occurred. The gaming centre implemented a strict BIOS update policy, ensuring that firmware upgrades were performed only when necessary and under controlled conditions.

Figure 2.6 illustrates the BIOS Flashback Process on a Motherboard, a crucial feature for updating or recovering BIOS firmware without requiring a fully operational system. The USB BIOS Flashback Port, highlighted in the image, allows users to update the motherboard firmware by simply inserting a USB drive containing the BIOS update file.

This process is beneficial in situations where the system fails to boot due to firmware corruption or hardware incompatibility. To perform a BIOS flashback, users must format a USB drive to FAT32, download the correct BIOS file from the manufacturer's website, rename it as per the instructions, insert it into the designated USB BIOS Flashback port, and press the BIOS Flashback button. The motherboard then updates the BIOS automatically, indicated by flashing LED lights.

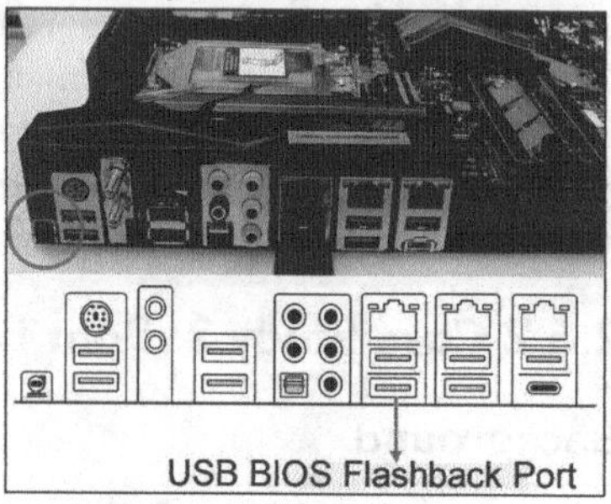

Figure 2.6: *BIOS Flashback Process on a Motherboard*

This feature enhances motherboard reliability and longevity by enabling firmware recovery without needing a functional CPU or RAM, making it a vital tool for troubleshooting and maintaining system stability.

2.6.3 Case Study 3: Overheating Issues in a High-Performance Workstation

Background

A graphic design and video editing firm noticed that several of their high-performance workstations were experiencing thermal throttling, resulting in slow rendering speeds and unexpected system crashes. The affected systems housed AMD Ryzen Threadripper processors and NVIDIA Quadro GPUs.

Engineers noticed that systems would freeze under heavy workloads, and temperature monitoring software revealed CPU temperatures exceeding 90°C, causing automatic clock speed reductions.

Diagnosis

An extensive **thermal inspection** revealed the following:

1. **Improperly Applied Thermal Paste:** The thermal paste application was uneven, leading to poor heat transfer between the CPU and heatsink.
2. **Clogged Heatsinks and Cooling Fans:** Layers of dust and debris were blocking airflow, reducing cooling efficiency.
3. **Inefficient Airflow Configuration:** The case fans were misconfigured, resulting in poor exhaust ventilation and hot air buildup inside the chassis.
4. **VRM Overheating:** The motherboard's voltage regulator module (VRM) overheated, affecting power stability for the CPU.

Solution Implemented

To prevent further overheating issues, the following steps were implemented:

- **Reapplying Thermal Paste:** Remove the old paste and apply a high-quality thermal compound for better heat conductivity.
- **Cleaning Cooling Components:** Conducted deep cleaning of heatsinks, cooling fans, and air vents to eliminate dust buildup.
- **Reconfiguring Airflow:** Installed additional exhaust fans and optimized airflow direction to create a proper positive pressure cooling system.
- **Installing VRM Heatsinks:** Added dedicated VRM cooling modules to stabilize power delivery.

After these optimizations, CPU temperatures dropped by 25°C, and the workstation operated at full capacity without thermal throttling or performance degradation.

Figure 2.7 illustrates the Correct Airflow Configuration for Cooling Optimization in a PC case, ensuring efficient heat dissipation and maintaining optimal system performance. The airflow setup consists of intake and outtake fans strategically positioned to promote proper ventilation.

Cool air is drawn in from the front intake fans and a side intake fan, directing fresh air toward critical components such as the graphics card and CPU. The heated air is then expelled through top and rear outtake fans, preventing heat buildup inside the case. The power supply unit (PSU) also contributes to airflow management by directing excess heat out of the case.

This configuration is essential for preventing overheating, improving hardware longevity, and maintaining stable system performance, especially in high-performance or gaming setups. Proper cable management and dust filters further enhance cooling efficiency, reducing the risk of thermal throttling.

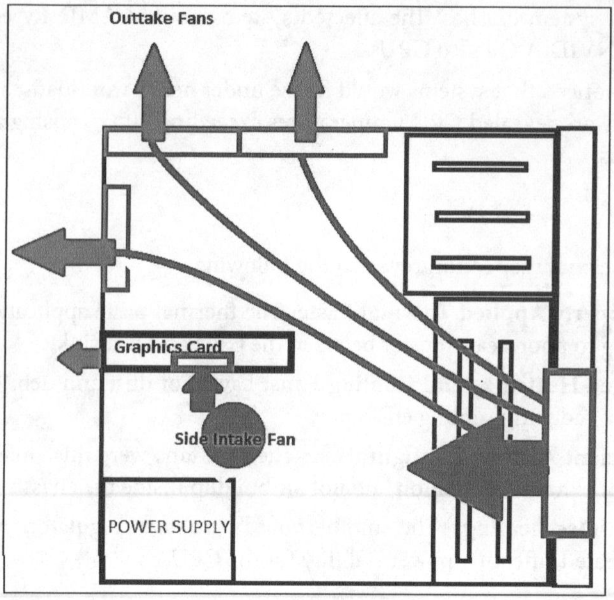

Figure 2.7: Correct Airflow Configuration for Cooling Optimization

Conclusion

Each case study demonstrates the importance of proactive motherboard maintenance and hardware optimization. Businesses and individual users can significantly improve system reliability by implementing power protection solutions, firmware update best practices, and efficient cooling strategies.

The next unit will explore Storage Devices and Data Interfaces, detailing their role in modern computing environments.

1. Interesting Facts

- **Real-World Impact:** Motherboard issues—whether power failures, firmware corruption, or thermal problems—can lead to significant productivity loss and operational disruptions.
- **Preventive Care Pays Off:** Regular maintenance and proactive diagnostics can reduce hardware failures and extend the lifespan of expensive IT assets.
- **Integrated Solutions:** Modern systems now incorporate features like dual BIOS chips, BIOS flashback utilities, and VRM heatsinks to help mitigate common problems.

2. Video Resources

- **Case Study Walkthroughs:** Look for videos with titles such as "Diagnosing Motherboard Power Failures" or "BIOS Corruption Recovery" for real-world troubleshooting examples.
- **Maintenance Best Practices:** Channels like *Linus Tech Tips* and *Techquickie* often cover hardware optimization techniques, including thermal management and proper PSU setup.

- **Expert Panels:** Webinars and roundtable discussions on IT maintenance strategies can provide broader insights into proactive system management.

3. Use of ICT in Maintenance

- **Diagnostic Software:** Tools like HWMonitor, SpeedFan, and built-in UEFI diagnostics help monitor system temperatures, voltages, and POST errors in real-time.
- **Remote Management:** Modern firmware allows remote troubleshooting and updates, which is crucial for managing large networks or enterprise systems.
- **Data Logging:** Continuous monitoring and logging of error codes and temperature trends can alert IT teams to potential issues before they lead to system failures.

4. Applications (Real Life / Industrial)

- **Business Environments:** Reliable motherboards are essential for companies to maintain workflow continuity. Proper maintenance minimizes downtime and protects critical data.
- **High-Performance Workstations:** In creative industries such as graphic design and video editing, optimized cooling and stable power delivery are crucial for rendering performance and system stability.
- **Enterprise and Industrial Systems:** Robust maintenance practices ensure that servers, control systems, and embedded devices run efficiently, reducing the need for costly replacements.

5. Detailed Case Studies and Best Practices

5.1 Case Study 1: Motherboard Power Failure in a Business Environment

Background

A mid-sized IT firm experienced recurring motherboard failures across more than 200 desktop systems. Employees reported random shutdowns and power cycling that disrupted daily operations.

Diagnosis

- **Unstable Power Supply** Frequent voltage fluctuations and power outages caused damaging surges.
- **Faulty Capacitors** Bulging or leaking capacitors indicated electrical stress and overheating.
- **Overloaded Power Strips:** Multiple high-power devices per strip led to excessive power draw.
- **Insufficient Cooling:** Dust buildup and poor ventilation stressed voltage regulators.

Solution Implemented

- **UPS Installation** Uninterruptible power supply systems were deployed at all workstations.

- **Capacitor Replacement** Replaced damaged capacitors with high-quality alternatives.
- **PSU Upgrade** Installed higher wattage, 80 Plus Gold certified power supplies.
- **Power Strip Management** Limited the number of high-power devices per strip and introduced regulated surge protectors.
- **Enhanced Airflow** Implemented scheduled cleaning and reorganized workstation setups.

Outcome A 70% reduction in motherboard failures within six months, leading to improved system reliability.

5.2 Case Study 2: Boot Failure Due to BIOS Corruption

Background

A high-end gaming PC at an eSports training centre failed to boot after a BIOS update was interrupted by a power failure. The system, featuring an Intel Core i9, 64GB RAM, and an RTX 4090 GPU, displayed no POST messages.

Diagnosis

- **Firmware Corruption** An incomplete BIOS update left the firmware unbootable.
- **No POST Indicators** Lack of beep codes or display output confirmed firmware failure.
- **CMOS Battery Failure** A drained battery prevented proper BIOS resets.
- **No Backup BIOS** The absence of a dual-BIOS feature meant there was no automatic recovery option.

Solution Implemented

- **BIOS Flashback** Used the motherboard's BIOS flashback utility with a USB drive containing fresh firmware.
- **CMOS Reset** Replaced the CMOS battery and reset BIOS settings via jumper pins.
- **Firmware Redundancy** Configured a secondary backup BIOS chip for future protection.
- **UPS Implementation** Ensured future BIOS updates occurred with UPS support to avoid power interruptions.

Outcome

The system was restored to normal operation with a strict BIOS update policy implemented to prevent recurrence.

5.3 Case Study 3: Overheating Issues in a High-Performance Workstation

Background

A graphic design and video editing firm experienced thermal throttling and unexpected crashes on workstations using AMD Ryzen Threadripper processors and NVIDIA Quadro GPUs. High CPU temperatures exceeded 90°C during intensive workloads.

Diagnosis

- **Thermal Paste Issues:** Uneven application led to poor heat transfer.
- **Clogged Cooling Components:** Dust buildup on heatsinks and fans reduced cooling efficiency.
- **Inefficient Airflow:** Misconfigured case fans prevented proper exhaust ventilation.
- **VRM Overheating:** Overheated Voltage Regulator Modules compromised power stability.

Solution Implemented

- **Thermal Paste Reapplication:** Removed old paste and applied high-quality thermal compound.
- **Deep Cleaning:** Thoroughly cleaned heatsinks, fans, and vents to remove dust.
- **Airflow Reconfiguration:** Added extra exhaust fans and optimized airflow to establish a positive-pressure cooling system.
- **VRM Cooling:** Installed dedicated VRM heatsinks to enhance power delivery stability.

Outcome

CPU temperatures dropped by 25°C, eliminating thermal throttling and improving overall performance.

SUMMARY

This unit explored the fundamental concepts related to motherboard architecture, functionality, and troubleshooting. The key topics covered include:

- **Motherboard Form Factors:** Comparison of AT, ATX, Micro-ATX, Mini-ATX, and other industry-standard motherboard designs.
- **Motherboard Components and Expansion Slots:** Detailed analysis of CPU sockets, RAM slots, chipsets, expansion slots (PCIe, PCI), and power connectors.
- **Motherboard Connectivity and Upgrading:** Understanding SATA, NVMe, USB, Thunderbolt, and next-gen connectivity options.
- **BIOS and UEFI Firmware:** Differences, advantages, and troubleshooting methods.
- **Common Motherboard Issues and Troubleshooting:** Diagnosing power failures, POST errors, overheating, and peripheral failures.
- **Case Studies and Best Practices:** Real-world examples of motherboard failures and maintenance strategies to improve longevity and performance.

EXERCISES

1. Subjective Questions (Conceptual and Analytical)

1. Explain the role of the motherboard in a computer system and describe its essential components.
2. Compare and contrast BIOS and UEFI firmware in terms of functionality, security, and update mechanisms.

3. Discuss different motherboard form factors and their impact on system design and expandability.
4. How do chipsets influence the performance and compatibility of a motherboard?
5. Describe PCIe slots and their role in high-performance computing.
6. What are the advantages and disadvantages of using NVMe storage over SATA?
7. Explain the significance of power management on a motherboard and how faulty power delivery can impact performance.
8. What are the common boot errors in a motherboard, and how can they be troubleshooted?
9. Describe a real-world scenario where a motherboard upgrade is necessary and outline the selection criteria.
10. Discuss the importance of cooling mechanisms and how VRMs play a role in temperature management.

2. Objective Questions (Multiple-Choice and True/False)

Multiple-choice questions (MCQs)

1. Which motherboard form factor is commonly used in compact desktops?
   (a) ATX (b) Micro-ATX
   (c) E-ATX (d) LPX
2. The Northbridge chipset primarily handles communication between the CPU and
   (a) Hard drives (b) RAM and PCIe devices
   (c) USB ports (d) Network controllers.
3. Which of the following is NOT a standard motherboard power connector?
   (a) 24-pin ATX (b) 8-pin EPS
   (c) 6-pin PCIe (d) 12V Battery Connector
4. BIOS firmware is stored in:
   (a) RAM (b) EEPROM
   (c) Hard Drive (d) GPU Memory
5. The primary benefit of PCIe Gen4 over PCIe Gen3 is
   (a) Lower power consumption (b) Higher bandwidth per lane
   (c) Compatibility with older GPUs (d) Improved LED support

True/False Questions

1. The motherboard chipset determines CPU and RAM compatibility. *(True/False)*
2. A UEFI firmware update can increase the performance of a processor. *(True/False)*
3. Overclocking a CPU increases heat output but does not affect power consumption. *(True/False)*
4. Thunderbolt ports are typically faster than standard USB 3.0 ports. *(True/False)*
5. BIOS settings can be reset by removing the CMOS battery. *(True/False)*

TEACHER'S KNOW MORE

For educators and advanced learners, additional resources and insights include

- **Advanced Chipset Design:** Understanding PCIe lane allocation and its impact on data transfer speeds.
- **Motherboard VRMs and Power Efficiency:** How voltage regulation modules influence CPU stability and overclocking potential.
- **Modern Security Features in UEFI:** Exploring Secure Boot, TPM integration, and firmware-level security measures.
- **Troubleshooting Lab Exercises:** Hands-on experiments diagnosing POST errors and BIOS failures.
- **Industry Trends in Motherboard Design:** Emerging technologies like AI-assisted cooling, PCIe 5.0, and DDR5 memory support.

This page is intentionally left blank!

3 UNIT

STORAGE DEVICES AND DATA INTERFACES

RATIONALE

Modern computer systems require reliable power delivery and advanced storage solutions to perform optimally. This unit explores two critical areas:

- **Power Supplies and Power Management:** Understanding the principles of power supplies—from modular designs to switching regulation—is essential for ensuring system stability and energy efficiency. Effective power management minimizes issues such as voltage fluctuations and overheating, which can damage components and reduce overall system lifespan.
- **Storage Devices and Their Evolution:** As data generation increases exponentially, storage technologies have evolved from magnetic and optical media to solid-state and cloud-based solutions. This unit covers the history, functionality, and future trends in storage, preparing students to evaluate and implement modern storage strategies that balance performance, capacity, and sustainability.

By examining both power and storage, students will gain insights into designing, troubleshooting, and upgrading computer systems—knowledge that is critical for careers in IT, hardware engineering, and systems management.

OUTCOMES

By the end of this unit, students will be able to:

- **Understand Power Supply Fundamentals:**
  - Explain the role of power supplies in computer systems.
  - Differentiate between modular and non-modular power supplies.
  - Describe switching regulations and evaluate efficiency considerations.
  - Identify common power issues and apply troubleshooting methods.
- **Trace the Evolution of Storage Devices:**
  - Describe the evolution of magnetic, optical, and solid-state storage technologies.
  - Explain the functionalities and differences between legacy storage devices (like floppy drives) and modern solutions (such as SSDs and NVMe).
  - Assess hybrid storage solutions and their applications.
- **Evaluate Legacy Storage Technologies:**
  - Understand the historical importance and obsolescence of floppy drives.
  - Analyze the transition from legacy storage to modern, high-performance storage systems.
- **Explore Advanced Storage Technologies:**
  - Explain RAID configurations and their role in data redundancy and performance.
  - Discuss cloud-based storage solutions and their benefits.

- Outline storage security and data recovery techniques.
- Examine future trends in data storage, preparing for emerging technologies in the field.

3.1 INTRODUCTION TO STORAGE TECHNOLOGIES

Overview of Storage Devices

Storage devices are fundamental to modern computing, enabling data storage, retrieval, and processing across various applications. These devices have evolved from mechanical drives to high-speed solid-state solutions, offering enhanced performance, durability, and efficiency.

Classification of Storage Technologies

Storage solutions are categorized based on their speed, volatility, and functionality into three main types:

1. Primary Storage (Volatile Memory)

Primary storage, also known as **volatile memory**, provides temporary storage for active processes. It ensures rapid data access but loses stored information when power is turned off.

- **Random Access Memory (RAM):** Temporary data storage for active applications.
- **Cache Memory:** High-speed storage within the CPU, minimizing data retrieval latency.
- **Registers:** Ultra-fast storage locations inside the CPU, managing immediate processing tasks.

2. Secondary Storage (Non-Volatile Memory)

Secondary storage retains data permanently, ensuring long-term storage solutions. Common examples include:

- **Hard Disk Drives (HDDs):** Mechanical spinning disks offering cost-effective bulk storage.
- **Solid-State Drives (SSDs):** NAND flash memory provides high-speed data transfer and enhanced durability.
- **Hybrid Drives (SSHDs):** Combining HDD capacity with SSD efficiency for optimized performance.

3. Tertiary Storage (Backup and Archival Storage)

Tertiary storage is dedicated to archiving, backup, and disaster recovery and is typically used in large-scale data centres and enterprises.

- **Optical Discs (CDs, DVDs, Blu-ray):** Physical media for long-term storage and distribution.
- **Magnetic Tape Drives:** Reliable, high-capacity storage for enterprise data archiving.
- **Cloud Storage:** Scalable, remote storage solutions offering accessibility and redundancy.

Table 3.1 compares HDDs and SSDs, highlighting differences in speed, durability, power consumption, cost, and use cases. SSDs offer faster data transfer speeds, more outstanding durability, and lower power consumption, making them ideal for high-performance computing and operating system installations. At the same time, HDDs remain a cost-effective solution for bulk storage and archival purposes.

***Table 3.1** :Comparison of HDDs and SSDs*

Feature	Hard Disk Drive (HD(d)	Solid-State Drive (SS(d)
Speed	Slower (100-200 MB/s)	Faster (500-7000 MB/s)
Durability	Mechanical parts prone to failure	No moving parts, highly durable
Power Consumption	Higher	Lower
Cost per GB	Lower	Higher
Use Cases	Bulk storage, archival	High-speed computing, OS installations

Figure 3.1 illustrates the Evolution of Storage Technologies, showcasing the transition from early mechanical storage solutions to modern high-speed digital storage.

The journey began with punched tape, one of the earliest forms of data storage, which relied on holes punched into paper strips to encode information. This was succeeded by magnetic tape, which provided greater storage capacity and reusability and was commonly used for backups and archival purposes. The introduction of the floppy disk revolutionized personal computing by offering portable and rewritable storage.

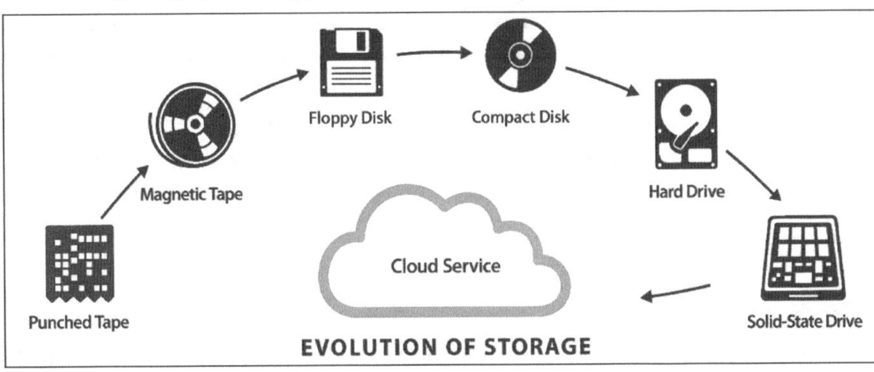

***Figure 3.1:** Evolution of Storage Technologies*

As technology advanced, compact disks (CDs) became the standard for digital media storage, followed by the hard disk drive (HD(d), which allowed for larger and faster access to data. The transition from mechanical storage to solid-state technology led to the development of solid-state drives (SSDs), which significantly improved speed, durability, and energy efficiency. In modern computing, cloud storage services now enable users to store and access data remotely, reducing reliance on physical storage devices while enhancing accessibility and scalability.

This evolution highlights the continuous improvement in data storage capacity, speed, and reliability, shaping the way digital information is managed today.

Storage Performance Metrics

Storage performance is evaluated based on multiple key parameters:

- **Read/Write Speeds:** Determines the efficiency of data retrieval and storage.
- **Latency:** Measures the delay before data transfer begins.
- **Endurance:** Defines the lifespan of a storage device, particularly in SSDs (measured in Terabytes Written - TBW).
- **Form Factor:** Refers to the physical size and connectivity type (e.g., 2.5" SATA, M.2, NVMe SSDs).

Conclusion

With rapid technological advancements, storage devices continue to evolve, delivering greater capacities, improved speeds, and enhanced reliability. Understanding the strengths and weaknesses of various storage solutions enables users to select the most suitable storage technology for their computing needs.

The following section will explore modern data interfaces, including SATA, NVMe, and PCIe, highlighting their role in high-speed data transfer.

3.2 MODERN DATA INTERFACES

Introduction to Data Interfaces

Data interfaces define the way storage devices communicate with other components in a computer system. Over time, storage interfaces have evolved to provide higher speeds, greater efficiency, and improved compatibility with modern hardware. These interfaces connect hard drives (HDDs), solid-state drives (SSDs), and external storage solutions to the motherboard, ensuring seamless data transfer.

The most commonly used modern data interfaces include SATA, NVMe, PCIe, USB, and Thunderbolt. Each interface is designed for specific applications, optimizing speed, power consumption, and overall system performance.

Serial ATA (SAT(a)

Overview

Serial ATA (SAT(a) is one of the most widely used storage interfaces for HDDs and SSDs. It replaced the older Parallel ATA (PAT(a) interface, offering higher speeds and better cable management.

Key Features of SATA

- Uses serial transmission for improved efficiency.
- Supports hot swapping, allowing devices to be connected or disconnected without shutting down the system.
- Utilizes a 7-pin data cable and a 15-pin power connector.
- It is commonly used for HDDs, SSDs, and optical drives.

Table 3.2 presents the different SATA versions and their respective data transfer rates, showcasing the evolution of SATA technology. SATA 1.0 provides a 1.5 Gbps transfer rate, while SATA 2.0 and SATA 3.0 significantly improve speeds, reaching 3.0 Gbps and 6.0 Gbps, respectively, enhancing storage performance and efficiency in modern computing.

Table 3.2: *SATA Versions and Performance:*

SATA Version	Data Transfer Rate
SATA 1.0	1.5 Gbps (150 MB/s)
SATA 2.0	3.0 Gbps (300 MB/s)
SATA 3.0	6.0 Gbps (600 MB/s)

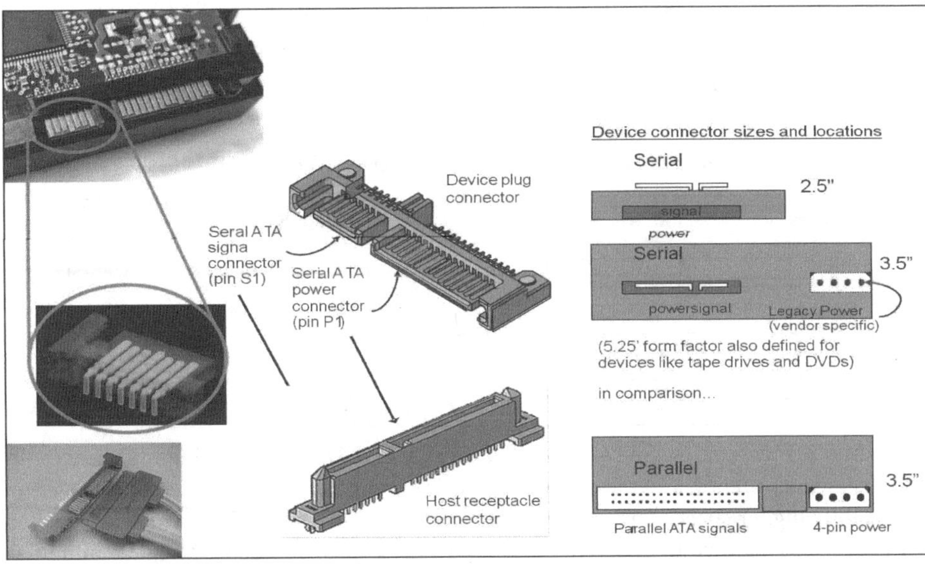

Figure 3.2: *SATA Interface and Connectors*

Figure 19 illustrates the SATA Interface and Connectors, showcasing the design and functionality of Serial ATA (SAT(a) connections used in modern storage devices.

SATA connectors consist of two primary components: the signal connector (pin S1) and the power connector (pin P1). The signal connector is responsible for data transmission between the storage device and the motherboard, while the power connector supplies the necessary voltage for operation. The host receptacle connector on the motherboard provides the interface for these connections.

The diagram also compares different device connector sizes. A 2.5-inch SATA connector is commonly used in laptops and SSDs, while a 3.5-inch SATA connector is typical for desktop HDDs and some enterprise storage solutions. Some legacy 3.5-inch devices may include additional 4-pin Molex power connectors for backward compatibility.

For comparison, the Parallel ATA (PAT(a) interface is also depicted, showing its wide 40-pin signal connector and 4-pin power plug, which was used in older HDDs and optical drives. The transition from PATA to SATA brought significant improvements in data transfer speeds, efficiency, and cable management, making SATA the industry standard for internal storage connections.

While SATA remains relevant for bulk storage solutions, newer interfaces like NVMe and PCIe offer significantly faster speeds for high-performance computing.

NVMe (Non-Volatile Memory Express)

Overview

NVMe is a high-performance storage interface designed for SSDs, offering much faster speeds compared to traditional SATA-based storage solutions. NVMe operates directly over PCIe lanes, reducing latency and increasing data transfer efficiency.

Key Features of NVMe

- It uses PCIe lanes to connect directly to the CPU for lower latency.
- Offers up to 7,000 MB/s read speeds, significantly faster than SATA SSDs.
- Supports multiple queues and parallel processing, improving efficiency for data-intensive applications.
- Available in M.2, U.2, and PCIe card formats.

Table 3.3: *Comparison: SATA SSD vs. NVMe SSD*

Feature	SATA SSD	NVMe SSD
Interface	SATA 3.0 (6.0 Gbps)	PCIe Gen3/Gen4
Speed	500-600 MB/s	Up to 7000 MB/s
Latency	Higher	Lower
Form Factor	2.5" Drive	M.2, U.2, PCIe Card

Table 3.3 compares SATA SSDs and NVMe SSDs, highlighting differences in interface, speed, latency, and form factor. NVMe SSDs utilize the PCIe interface, delivering significantly higher speeds and lower latency compared to SATA SSDs, which are limited by the 6.0 Gbps bandwidth of SATA 3.0. NVMe SSDs come in compact M.2, U.2, and PCIe card form factors, making them ideal for high-performance computing and gaming.

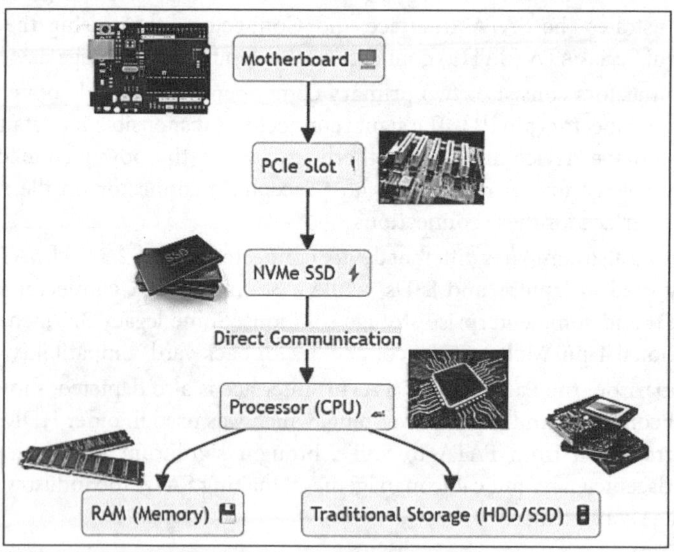

Figure 3.3: *NVMe SSD and PCIe Slot Connection*

Figure 3.3 illustrates the NVMe SSD and PCIe Slot Connection, demonstrating the high-speed data transfer pathway between storage and the processor.

The motherboard hosts the PCIe slot, where the NVMe SSD is installed. Unlike traditional SATA SSDs, NVMe drives leverage the PCIe interface to provide direct communication with the CPU, bypassing bottlenecks associated with older storage interfaces. This significantly enhances read/write speeds, reducing data latency and improving system performance.

Once connected, the processor (CPU) interacts directly with the NVMe SSD for rapid data retrieval and storage operations. The CPU also manages interactions with RAM (Memory) for active processing tasks and traditional storage (HDD/SS(d) for long-term data retention.

This architecture optimizes computing efficiency, making NVMe SSDs ideal for gaming, high-performance computing, and enterprise applications requiring fast and reliable storage solutions.

NVMe SSDs are widely used in gaming, video editing, AI workloads, and enterprise-level computing, where speed and efficiency are critical.

PCIe (Peripheral Component Interconnect Express)

Overview

PCIe is a high-speed expansion bus that connects storage devices, graphics cards, and other peripherals directly to the CPU. Modern storage solutions such as NVMe SSDs utilize PCIe lanes for ultra-fast data transmission.

Key Features of PCIe

- Provides dedicated lanes (x1, x4, x8, x16) for efficient data transfer.
- Supports multiple generations (PCIe Gen3, Gen4, and Gen5), each offering increased bandwidth.
- Used in NVMe SSDs, GPUs, network adapters, and AI accelerators.

Table 3.4: *PCIe Speed Comparisons:*

PCIe Generation	Bandwidth per Lane	Total Bandwidth (x16)
PCIe Gen3	8 GT/s	128 GB/s
PCIe Gen4	16 GT/s	256 GB/s
PCIe Gen5	32 GT/s	512 GB/s

Table 3.4 presents PCIe Speed Comparisons, outlining bandwidth improvements across different PCIe generations. With each successive generation, PCIe bandwidth per lane doubles, allowing for higher data transfer speeds. PCIe Gen3 provides 8 GT/s per lane, while Gen4 and Gen5 significantly increase speeds to 16 GT/s and 32 GT/s, making them essential for high-performance GPUs, NVMe SSDs, and data-intensive applications.

PCIe continues to be the preferred interface for high-performance applications, enabling low-latency, high-bandwidth communication between storage devices and the CPU.

USB and Thunderbolt Interfaces for External Storage

USB (Universal Serial Bus)

USB is the **most common interface for external storage devices,** including **flash drives, external HDDs, and SSDs.** The latest versions provide faster speeds and improved power efficiency.

Table 3.5 compares USB versions and their respective data transfer speeds, showcasing the evolution of USB technology. USB 2.0 offers a maximum speed of 480 Mbps, while USB 3.0 and 3.1 Gen2 significantly improve data rates to 5 Gbps and 10 Gbps, respectively. The latest USB 4.0 standard reaches 40 Gbps, making it ideal for high-speed data transfer, external storage, and advanced peripherals.

Table 3.5: *Comparison of USB Versions and Data Transfer Speeds*

USB Version	Data Transfer Speed
USB 2.0	480 Mbps (60 MB/s)
USB 3.0	5 Gbps (625 MB/s)
USB 3.1 Gen2	10 Gbps (1250 MB/s)
USB 4.0	40 Gbps

Figure 3.4 illustrates USB Ports and Connector Types, comparing the structural differences between USB 2.0 and USB 3.0 standards.

USB connectors are categorized based on their form factor and function. The USB 2.0 standard features different connector types, including A Female, A Male, B Male, and Micro B Male, which are commonly used in external storage devices, printers, and mobile phones.

In contrast, USB 3.0 introduces an improved design with additional pins for faster data transfer rates, denoted by the SS (SuperSpee(d) symbol. The USB 3.0 A Male and Female connectors maintain backward compatibility with USB 2.0 but offer significantly higher bandwidth. The USB 3.0 B Male and Micro B Male connectors feature an extended pin layout, distinguishing them from their USB 2.0 counterparts.

These advancements in USB technology enhance data transfer speeds, power efficiency, and overall connectivity, making USB 3.0 the preferred choice for high-speed external storage devices and peripherals.

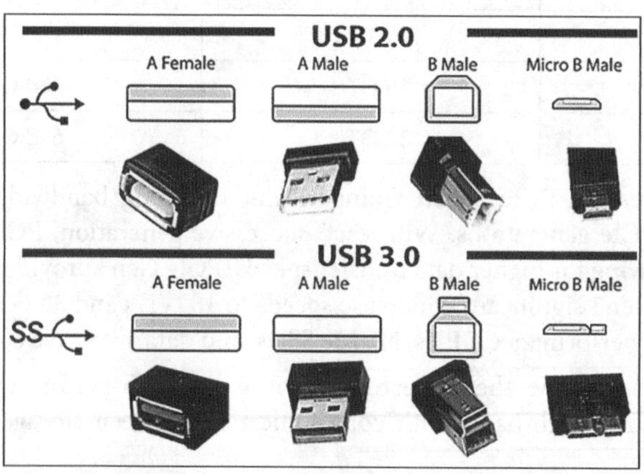

Figure 3.4: *USB Ports and Connector Types*

Thunderbolt

Thunderbolt is an advanced data transfer interface developed by Intel and Apple, primarily used in high-speed external SSDs, docking stations, and display connections.

- Thunderbolt 3 & 4 offer up to 40 Gbps speeds, ideal for high-performance storage.
- Supports USB-C connectors, improving compatibility with modern laptops and desktops.
- Enables daisy-chaining of multiple devices through a single port.

Figure 3.5: Thunderbolt Connectivity in External SSDs

Figure 3.5 illustrates Thunderbolt Connectivity in External SSDs, highlighting the high-speed data transfer capabilities between storage devices and computers.

Thunderbolt technology, developed by Intel and Apple, provides lightning-fast data transfer speeds and supports daisy-chaining multiple peripherals through a single port. In the image, an external SSD is connected to a laptop using a Thunderbolt cable, enabling high-bandwidth communication that is ideal for tasks such as video editing, large file transfers, and gaming.

Compared to traditional USB connections, Thunderbolt offers higher throughput, lower latency, and power delivery capabilities, making it a preferred choice for professionals working with large datasets and high-performance storage solutions. With advancements in Thunderbolt 3 and 4, users benefit from USB-C compatibility, faster read/write speeds, and enhanced connectivity options, ensuring seamless data access across multiple devices.

Conclusion

Modern data interfaces have revolutionized storage technology, providing faster speeds, lower latency, and enhanced efficiency. While SATA remains a viable option for cost-effective storage, NVMe and PCIe have become the standard for high-speed computing applications.

External storage solutions continue to improve with USB 4.0 and Thunderbolt, allowing for fast, portable, and high-capacity storage options.

The following section will discuss RAID (Redundant Array of Independent Disks) and its role in data redundancy, performance enhancement, and fault tolerance.

Interesting Facts

- **Evolution at Lightning Speed:** Storage technologies have evolved from bulky, slow mechanical drives (HDDs) to ultra-fast, durable solid-state drives (SSDs) and cloud storage, reflecting a dramatic shift in how we access and manage data.
- **Tiny Yet Mighty:** Modern SSDs in the M.2 form factor can be smaller than a credit card yet deliver read speeds up to 7,000 MB/s—showcasing the power of miniaturization.
- **Data Explosion:** With global data expected to grow exponentially, storage devices not only save our files but also enable innovations like big data analytics, AI, and IoT.

Video Resources

- **Storage Evolution Explained:** Look for videos titled "The Evolution of Storage Devices" or "From HDD to SSD: What has Changed?" on platforms like YouTube for animated timelines and expert insights.
- **Interface Deep Dives:** Search for "How NVMe SSDs Work" or "Understanding PCIe and SATA" to get a visual explanation of how these interfaces revolutionize data transfer.
- **DIY Projects:** Channels like *Linus Tech Tips* and *Techquickie* offer tutorials on upgrading storage, optimizing performance, and even building our own NAS.

Use of ICT

- **Real-Time Monitoring:** ICT tools like HWMonitor, CrystalDiskInfo, and UEFI-based diagnostics enable users to monitor storage health, track read/write speeds, and forecast device endurance.
- **Cloud Integration:** Modern ICT systems leverage cloud storage to synchronize data across devices, ensuring that data is accessible anytime, anywhere while maintaining redundancy.
- **Data Security:** Encryption technologies and secure data transfer protocols protect sensitive information during transmission between storage devices and the cloud.

Applications (Real Life/Industrial)

- **Everyday Computing:** For consumers, SSDs in laptops and desktops mean faster boot times, smoother multimedia editing, and an overall responsive computing experience.
- **Enterprise Solutions:** Data centres rely on high-capacity HDDs and NVMe SSDs to manage vast amounts of data, supporting everything from financial transactions to healthcare records.
- **Industrial Automation:** Manufacturing plants and smart cities use robust storage solutions to log sensor data, run real-time analytics, and maintain operational integrity under harsh conditions.

Case Study: Environmental/Sustainability/Social/Ethical Issues

Context

In today's data-driven world, storage devices contribute significantly to electronic waste (e-waste). Responsible management and sustainable practices in the storage industry are vital for reducing environmental impact.

Scenario

- **A major cloud service provider embarked on a "Green Storage Initiative" aimed at reducing the ecological footprint of its data centres:**
  - **Eco-Friendly Materials:** Transitioned to using recyclable materials in SSD production and adopted energy-efficient designs.
  - **Efficient Cooling:** Implemented advanced cooling techniques that reduce energy consumption and extend the lifespan of storage devices.

   - **Recycling Programs:** Established partnerships with recycling companies to reclaim valuable components from decommissioned drives, lowering e-waste and promoting a circular economy.

Discussion Points

- How can sustainable design and energy efficiency in storage technologies help combat climate change?
- What role do consumers and businesses play in encouraging environmentally responsible practices in the tech industry?
- In what ways could emerging storage technologies further reduce the environmental impact of data centres?

Creating Inquisitiveness and Curiosity

- **Open-Ended Questions:**
   - What might storage devices look like in 20 years, and how could quantum storage or DNA-based storage revolutionize data retention?
   - How does the interplay between speed, durability, and cost influence the design of future storage solutions?
   - Can you imagine new data interfaces that might replace or enhance today's SATA, NVMe, or PCIe standards?
- **Challenge Projects** Encourage learners to design a "green data centre" plan that incorporates sustainable storage solutions and energy-efficient cooling systems or create a comparative study of storage performance in various real-world scenarios.

Solved Problems (With Increasing Difficulty Level)

Problem 1 (Basic)

Question

What is the primary difference between an HDD and an SSD?

Solution

An HDD uses mechanical spinning disks and read/write heads to store data, while an SSD uses NAND flash memory with no moving parts, offering faster read/write speeds and higher durability.

Problem 2 (Intermediate)

Question

Compare SATA and NVMe interfaces in terms of speed and latency.

Solution

SATA Interface: Typically offers speeds up to 600 MB/s with higher latency due to its older protocol designed for HDDs and early SSDs.

- **NVMe Interface:** Operates over PCIe lanes, enabling speeds up to 7,000 MB/s with much lower latency, making it ideal for high-performance applications.

Problem 3 (Advanced)

Question

How do form factors and endurance affect the choice between different SSD types for a high-performance workstation?

Solution

- **Form Factor:** M.2 NVMe SSDs are compact and offer high speeds, which are ideal for space-constrained, performance-intensive workstations.
- **Endurance:** Measured in Terabytes Written (TBW), higher endurance SSDs ensure that frequent read/write operations do not prematurely wear out the device—crucial for tasks like video editing or database management.

Problem 4 (Challenging)

Question

Discuss how the integration of cloud storage and local high-speed storage can be optimized for a small business looking to balance performance, cost, and data security.

Solution

- **Local High-Speed Storage:** Use NVMe SSDs for critical, high-performance tasks (e.g., operating systems, applications, and frequently accessed dat(a) to ensure rapid response times.
- **Cloud Storage Integration:** Store large datasets, backups, and less frequently accessed information in the cloud to provide scalability, redundancy, and remote access.
- **Data Security:** Implement encryption for both local and cloud storage and use data synchronization tools that ensure seamless updates and backups, balancing immediate performance needs with long-term reliability and disaster recovery.

3.3 RAID (REDUNDANT ARRAY OF INDEPENDENT DISKS)

Introduction to RAID

RAID (Redundant Array of Independent Disks) is a data storage virtualization technology that combines multiple physical disk drives into a single logical unit to enhance performance, reliability, and fault tolerance. Developed initially to mitigate storage failures and data loss, RAID is widely used in enterprise servers, high-performance workstations, and data centres.

RAID configurations vary based on their approach to data striping, mirroring, and parity, with each RAID level providing distinct advantages in speed, redundancy, or both.

Types of RAID Configurations

RAID levels are categorized based on how they distribute data and redundancy across drives. The most commonly used RAID levels include RAID 0, RAID 1, RAID 5, RAID 6, and RAID 10.

RAID 0 (Striping – Performance-Only, No Redundancy)

- Data is split (stripe(d) across multiple drives, increasing read and write speeds.
- No redundancy – If one drive fails, all data is lost.
- Best for: High-speed applications where redundancy is not a priority (e.g., gaming, video editing).

Table 3.6 outlines the RAID 0 Configuration and Performance Characteristics, highlighting its advantages and limitations. RAID 0 provides very high read and write speeds by stripping data across multiple drives, but it lacks redundancy. As a result, if a single drive fails, all data is lost, making it suitable for high-speed applications but not for critical data storage.

***Table 3.6:** RAID 0 Configuration and Performance Characteristics*

Feature	RAID 0
Minimum Disks Required	2
Redundancy	None
Read Speed	Very High
Write Speed	Very High
Fault Tolerance	None – Single drive failure results in complete data loss

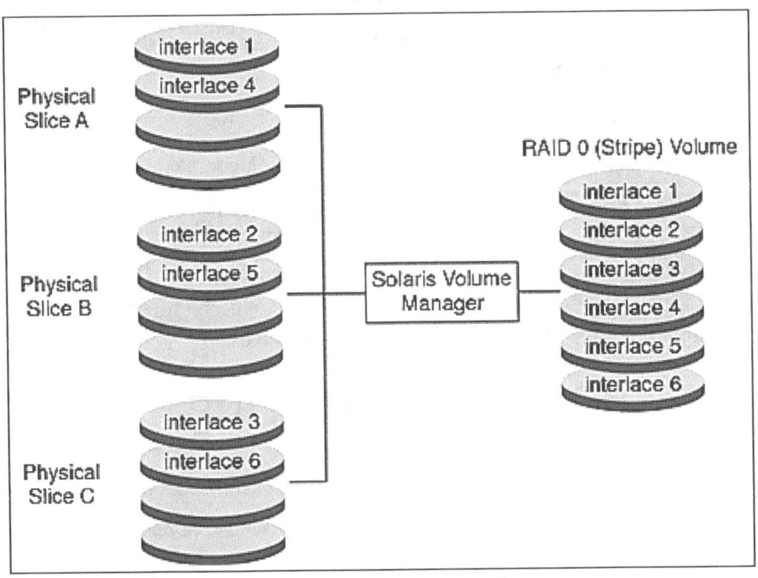

***Figure 3.6:** RAID 0 Striping Process*

Figure 3.6 illustrates the RAID 0 Striping Process, demonstrating how data is distributed across multiple physical storage devices to enhance performance.

RAID 0, also known as striping, divides data into smaller chunks called interlaces, which are then written sequentially across multiple disks. In this diagram, three physical storage slices (A, B, and (c) contain different interlaced data segments that the Solaris Volume Manager manages. The system reorganizes these interlaces into a unified RAID 0 volume, where the data is striped evenly across all available disks.

This striping technique significantly improves read and write speeds by allowing simultaneous access to multiple disks. It is ideal for applications that require high performance, such as gaming, video editing, and large-scale data processing. However, RAID 0 does not provide fault tolerance—if one disk fails, all data within the array is lost, emphasizing the need for regular backups when using this configuration.

RAID 1 (Mirroring – Data Redundancy, No Performance Boost)

- **Duplicates (mirrors) data** across two or more drives.
- **Excellent fault tolerance** – One drive can fail without losing data.
- **There is no increase in write speeds**, but read speeds can improve.
- **Best for:** Critical applications requiring data integrity, such as financial records.

Table 3.7 outlines the RAID 1 Configuration and Fault Tolerance Features, emphasizing its data protection benefits. RAID 1 uses mirroring, where data is duplicated across two drives, ensuring 100% redundancy. While read speed is moderate, write speed is lower since data must be written to both drives simultaneously. This configuration provides high fault tolerance, allowing continued operation even if one drive fails, making it ideal for critical data storage and system reliability.

***Table 3.7:** RAID 1 Configuration and Fault Tolerance Features*

Feature	RAID 1
Minimum Disks Required	2
Redundancy	100%
Read Speed	Moderate
Write Speed	Lower (same as a single drive)
Fault Tolerance	High – Data remains accessible if one drive fails.

Figure 3.7 illustrates the RAID 1 Mirroring Process, which enhances data redundancy by creating identical copies of information across two drives.

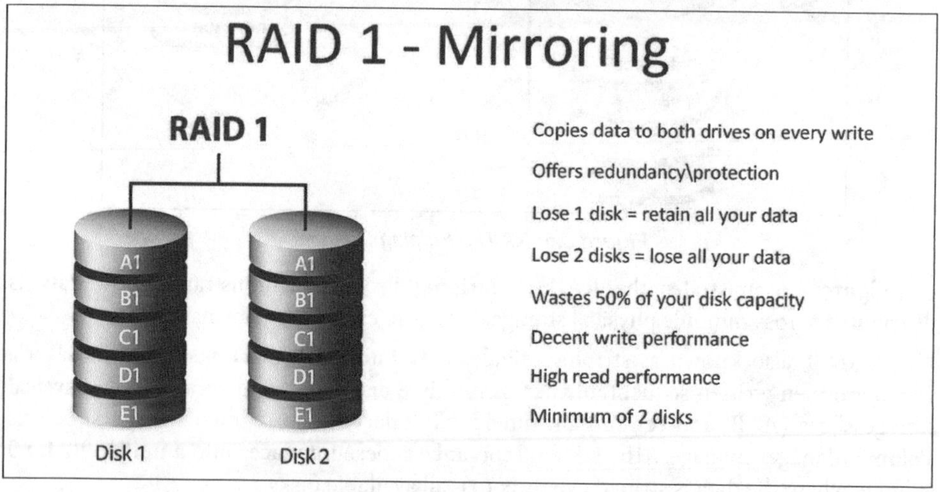

***Figure 3.7:** RAID 1 Mirroring Process*

In this configuration, Disk 1 and Disk 2 store identical copies of data blocks (A1, B1, C1, etc.), ensuring fault tolerance. Every write operation is mirrored simultaneously on both disks, so if one drive fails, the other continues functioning without data loss. This setup offers high data protection but results in 50% storage efficiency, as the usable space is limited to the capacity of a single disk.

RAID 1 provides high read performance since data can be read from either disk, while write performance remains decent due to the duplication process. A minimum of two disks is required, and both must have equal storage capacity to ensure seamless operation. This mirroring technique is ideal for critical data storage, financial systems, and business environments where data integrity and reliability are top priorities.

RAID 5 (Striping with Distributed Parity – Performance + Redundancy)

- **Combines striping with distributed parity**, providing both speed and data protection.
- If a single drive fails, the system can **rebuild data using parity information**.
- More storage-efficient than RAID 1.
- **Best for:** Enterprise servers, database systems, and high-availability environments.

Table 3.8 outlines the RAID 5 Configuration and Data Redundancy Features, highlighting its balance between performance and fault tolerance. RAID 5 uses striping with parity, allowing for high read speeds and moderate write speeds while maintaining fault tolerance. If a single drive fails, data can be reconstructed using parity information, making it a cost-effective and reliable option for data storage in servers and enterprise environments.

Table 3.8: *RAID 5 Configuration and Data Redundancy Features*

Feature	RAID 5
Minimum Disks Required	3
Redundancy	Parity-based (1 drive can fail)
Read Speed	High
Write Speed	Moderate
Fault Tolerance	Good – Data can be rebuilt if one drive fails

RAID 5

Right Asynchronous

Disk 0	Disk 1	Disk 2	Disk 3
Parity	0	1	2
3	Parity	4	5
6	7	Parity	8
9	10	11	Parity

Figure 3.8: *RAID 5 Parity Calculation*

Figure 3.8 illustrates the RAID 5 Parity Calculation, demonstrating how data and parity information are distributed across multiple disks to ensure fault tolerance and redundancy.

RAID 5 uses striping with parity method, where data is divided across at least three disks, with parity blocks rotating across different drives instead of being stored on a single disk. In this example, each row represents a stripe, with parity data (marked as "Parity") calculated and stored on different disks per stripe. The parity is used to reconstruct data in the event of a disk failure, allowing the system to continue operating with minimal disruption.

This configuration provides better storage efficiency than RAID 1, as only one disk's worth of space is used for redundancy, regardless of the total number of drives. RAID 5 is ideal for servers, database storage, and high-read environments, offering a balance of performance, redundancy, and capacity. However, write operations may be slower due to the need for parity calculations, and performance can degrade during recovery from a disk failure.

RAID 6 (Striping with Double Parity – Enhanced Fault Tolerance)

- Similar to RAID 5, it stores **two sets of parity data**, allowing for the failure of **up to two drives.**
- **Higher write overhead** due to dual parity calculations.
- **Best for:** Mission-critical applications that require **maximum fault tolerance.**

***Table 3.9:** RAID 6 Configuration and Fault Tolerance Features*

Feature	RAID 6
Minimum Disks Required	4
Redundancy	Two-drive failure tolerance
Read Speed	High
Write Speed	Lower than RAID 5 (due to extra parity calculations)
Fault Tolerance	Very High – The system survived two drive failures.

Table 3.9 outlines the RAID 6 Configuration and Fault Tolerance Features, emphasizing its enhanced data protection capabilities. RAID 6 utilizes striping with dual parity, allowing the system to withstand the failure of two drives simultaneously. It offers high read speeds, but write speeds are lower than RAID 5 due to the additional parity calculations. This configuration provides very high fault tolerance, making it ideal for enterprise storage, mission-critical applications, and data centres requiring maximum reliability.

Figure 3.9 illustrates the RAID 6 Data Striping and Dual Parity mechanism, which enhances fault tolerance by distributing data and parity information across multiple disks.

RAID 6 is an extension of RAID 5, incorporating dual parity blocks (P1 and P2) that allow the system to withstand two simultaneous disk failures without data loss. Each stripe contains data blocks (A, B, C, etc.) spread across different disks, while two independent parity calculations (P1 and P2) are stored in separate locations. This redundancy significantly improves data reliability and makes RAID 6 ideal for high-availability systems, enterprise storage, and mission-critical applications.

Although RAID 6 provides superior fault tolerance compared to RAID 5, it requires at least four disks and results in reduced write performance due to the additional parity computations. However, the trade-off is excellent data protection, making it a preferred choice for environments where data integrity and uptime are crucial.

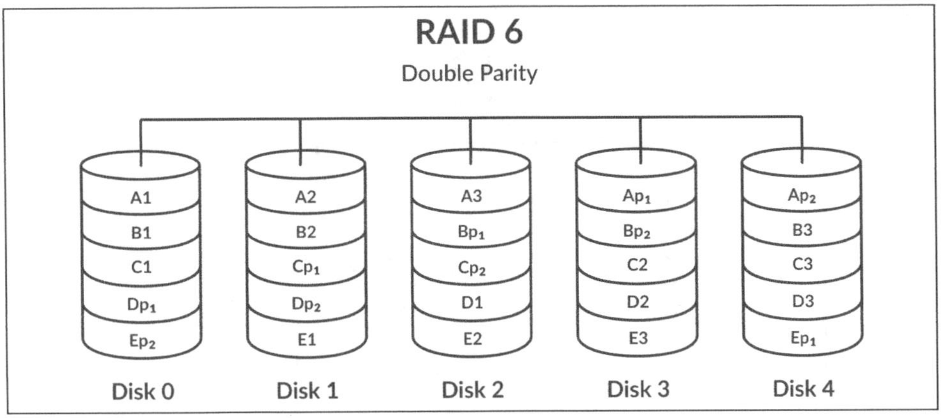

Figure 3.9: *RAID 6 Data Striping and Dual Parity*

RAID 10 (Striping + Mirroring – High Performance and Redundancy)

- Combines RAID 1 (mirroring) and RAID 0 (striping) to provide both high performance and redundancy.
- Requires at least four drives, where pairs of drives are mirrored and striped.
- Best for: High-performance enterprise applications requiring speed and data security.

Table 3.10 outlines the RAID 10 Configuration and Performance Characteristics, combining the benefits of RAID 1 (mirroring) and RAID 0 (striping). RAID 10 offers very high read and write speeds while ensuring high fault tolerance by mirroring data across pairs of drives. At least one drive from each mirrored pair must survive for data integrity to be maintained, making RAID 10 an ideal choice for high-performance applications that require both speed and redundancy, such as databases and enterprise storage solutions.

Table 3.10 *RAID 10 Configuration and Performance Characteristics*

Feature	RAID 10
Minimum Disks Required	4
Redundancy	Full mirroring of data
Read Speed	Very High
Write Speed	High
Fault Tolerance	High – At least one drive from each mirrored pair must survive

Figure 3.10 illustrates the RAID 10 Configuration, which combines mirroring (RAID 1) and striping (RAID 0) to enhance both performance and fault tolerance.

RAID 10 requires a minimum of four disks, where data is first mirrored (duplicate(d) across two disks and then striped (split) across mirrored pairs. In this configuration, each data block (A1, A2, A3, etc.) is stored on two separate drives, ensuring redundancy. This setup provides high-speed read and write performance, as data can be accessed from multiple disks simultaneously while also offering protection against disk failure—as long as at least one disk in each mirrored pair remains functional.

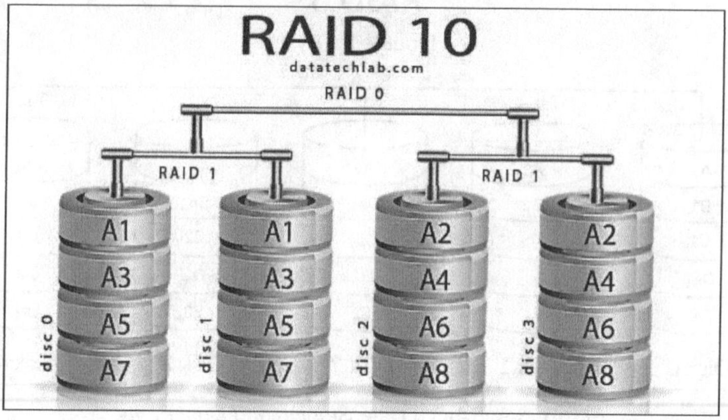

Figure 3.10: *RAID 10 Configuration*

RAID 10 is ideal for high-performance applications such as database management, financial transactions, and enterprise-level storage, where both speed and data integrity are critical. However, the trade-off is that 50% of storage capacity is lost to mirroring, making it a costly yet reliable solution for businesses requiring minimal downtime and high data availability.

Table 3.11: *Comparison of RAID Levels*

RAID Level	Min Disks	Redundancy	Read Speed	Write Speed	Fault Tolerance
RAID 0	2	None	Very High	Very High	None
RAID 1	2	100%	Moderate	Low	High (1 drive failure)
RAID 5	3	Parity-Based	High	Moderate	Good (1 drive failure)
RAID 6	4	Dual Parity	High	Lower	Very High (2 drive failures)
RAID 10	4	Mirrored + Striped	Very High	High	High (mirrored redundancy)

Table 3.11 provides a comparison of different RAID levels, highlighting their requirements, redundancy, performance, and fault tolerance. RAID 0 offers high speed but no redundancy, while RAID 1 provides full mirroring for data protection. RAID 5 and RAID 6 utilize parity for fault tolerance, with RAID 6 allowing for dual-drive failure protection. RAID 10 combines mirroring and striping, offering both high performance and redundancy, making it an ideal choice for critical data storage and high-speed applications.

Advantages and Disadvantages of RAID

Advantages

- **Improved Performance**: RAID **boosts read/write speeds** in striped configurations (RAID 0, RAID 10).

- **Fault Tolerance**: Redundant setups **prevent data loss** in case of drive failure (RAID 1, RAID 5, RAID 6).
- **Better Storage Management**: Combines multiple smaller drives into one logical volume.
- **Scalability**: Many RAID configurations can be expanded with additional drives.

Disadvantages

- **Higher Cost**: RAID requires multiple drives, increasing hardware expenses. ✗ Complexity – Setup and management require technical expertise.
- **Write Penalty in Parity-Based RAID**: RAID 5 and RAID 6 have slower write speeds due to parity calculations.
- **Not a Substitute for Backups**: While RAID offers redundancy, data corruption or accidental deletion still requires backups.

Conclusion

RAID technology plays a crucial role in data protection, system performance, and redundancy. Organizations choose different RAID levels based on their specific storage requirements, balancing performance, cost, and fault tolerance. While RAID enhances reliability, it is not a substitute for regular backups—a comprehensive data protection strategy should include both RAID and offsite backups.

The following section will discuss storage security and encryption, exploring methods to safeguard sensitive data against unauthorized access and cyber threats.

Interesting Facts

- **Data Protection & Performance** RAID technology was initially developed to both boost performance and protect data by distributing it across multiple drives. Some configurations (like RAID 5 and RAID 6) can even rebuild data automatically if one or two drives fail.
- **Versatility** There are various RAID levels—from RAID 0, which focuses purely on speed with no redundancy, to RAID 10, which offers both speed and data mirroring. This versatility makes RAID a key component in both high-performance and mission-critical environments.
- **Adoption Across Industries:** RAID is a backbone technology in data centres, enterprise servers, and high-end workstations, ensuring that systems remain operational even in the event of hardware failures.

Video Resources

- **Explainer Videos:** Look for titles like "RAID Levels Explained – RAID 0, RAID 1, RAID 5, RAID 6, and RAID 10" on YouTube for animated breakdowns of how each level works.
- **Tutorials & Setup Guides:** Videos such as "How to Configure RAID on Your PC" or "RAID Setup in Windows/Linux" provide step-by-step instructions.
- **Expert Discussions:** Channels like *Linus Tech Tips* and *Techquickie* often discuss the pros and cons of different RAID configurations in real-world scenarios.

Use of ICT

- **Robust Data Management:** In ICT environments, RAID arrays are essential for creating fault-tolerant and high-performance storage systems. They are widely used in servers and cloud infrastructures to ensure uninterrupted service and data availability.
- **Real-Time Monitoring:** Advanced RAID controllers come with software that monitors disk health, performance, and error logs, enabling IT professionals to predict and preempt hardware issues.
- **Virtualization & Cloud Integration:** RAID is often integrated into virtualized environments, where data redundancy and rapid access speeds are critical for managing large-scale, distributed systems.

Applications (Real Life/Industrial)

- **Enterprise Data Centers:** RAID configurations such as RAID 5 and RAID 6 are standard in data centres to ensure high availability and data protection for critical applications.
- **High-Performance Workstations:** Professionals in video editing, 3D rendering, and gaming often use RAID 0 or RAID 10 setups to maximize speed and performance.
- **Industrial Control Systems:** In manufacturing and automation, RAID arrays protect system integrity by ensuring that control data is not lost, even if individual drives fail.
- **Small Business Servers:** Many small to medium-sized enterprises deploy RAID systems to safeguard financial records, customer data, and other vital information against drive failures.

Case Study (Environmental/Sustainability/Social/Ethical Issues)

Context

A municipal data centre faced frequent hardware failures and high levels of electronic waste due to outdated storage systems. They aimed to improve system resilience and reduce their environmental footprint.

Scenario

- **Challenge:** The centre was replacing failed drives regularly, contributing to significant e-waste and increased energy consumption.
- **Solution:**
  - They implemented RAID 5 across multiple servers, which uses distributed parity to allow the system to rebuild data automatically if one drive fails.
  - By selecting energy-efficient drives and optimizing storage performance, the data centre reduced the number of drive replacements and cut overall power consumption.
  - Additionally, the centre established a recycling program for decommissioned drives, recovering valuable materials and reducing landfill waste.

Discussion Points

- How does implementing a fault-tolerant RAID configuration help reduce electronic waste?
- What are the ethical responsibilities of organizations in managing their technology sustainably?
- Can integrating energy-efficient storage solutions positively impact both operational costs and the environment?

Create Inquisitiveness and Curiosity

- **Future Possibilities:** How might future storage technologies, such as NVMe over Fabrics or even quantum storage, transform RAID architectures?
- **Design Challenges:** If we are tasked with designing a RAID system for a mission-critical application in an extreme environment (such as space or deep-sea exploration), what factors would you prioritize?
- **Debate:** In which scenarios might sacrifice redundancy for higher performance (as in RAID 0) be acceptable, and what risks would that entail?
- **Innovation Brainstorm:** Can we imagine a new RAID level that optimally balances performance, cost, and environmental impact? What would its key features be?

Solved Problems (With Increasing Difficulty Level)

Problem 1 (Basic)

Question

What is the main purpose of RAID 1, and what is its minimum disk requirement?

Solution

RAID 1 provides data redundancy through mirroring, ensuring that an exact copy of the data is stored on two or more disks. The minimum requirement is two disks.

Problem 2 (Intermediate)

Question

Explain how RAID 5 achieves a balance between performance and redundancy. What is the minimum number of disks needed for RAID 5?

Solution

RAID 5 strips data across multiple disks and uses distributed parity to provide fault tolerance. If one disk fails, the data can be reconstructed using the parity information. A minimum of 3 disks is required.

Problem 3 (Advanced)

Question

Compare RAID 6 and RAID 10 in terms of fault tolerance and write performance. What trade-offs would a system designer need to consider?

Solution

- **RÀID 6:** Utilizes double parity, allowing for up to 2 drive failures. However, the extra parity calculations can reduce write speeds.
- **RAID 10:** Combines striping (RAID 0) and mirroring (RAID 1), providing excellent read/write performance and fault tolerance, but it requires more disks (minimum 4) and sacrifices storage efficiency.

The designer must weigh the need for maximum fault tolerance (RAID 6) against higher write performance and simpler rebuilds (RAID 10), as well as cost and storage efficiency.

Problem 4 (Challenging)

Question

A small business needs to protect critical data while also maintaining high read speeds for daily operations. They have a budget constraint that limits the number of disks they can use. Propose a RAID configuration, justify our choice, and explain any potential risks.

Solution

A viable solution is to use RAID 5:

- **Justification**
    - **Cost-Effective:** RAID 5 requires a minimum of 3 disks, which balances cost and redundancy.
    - **Fault Tolerance:** It protects against a single drive failure through parity.
    - **Performance:** It offers high read speeds that are suitable for daily operations.
- **Potential Risks:**
    - **Write Penalty:** RAID 5 has slower write speeds due to parity calculations, which may affect performance if write operations are intensive.
    - **Rebuild Stress:** In the event of a drive failure, the rebuild process can put stress on the remaining disks, potentially leading to another failure if the drives are old.

Implementing regular backups and monitoring the health of the drives can mitigate these risks.

3.4 STORAGE SECURITY AND ENCRYPTION

Introduction to Storage Security

In the digital era, data security has become a critical concern for individuals, enterprises, and governments. With the increasing amount of sensitive information stored on local devices, cloud systems, and enterprise servers, it is imperative to implement strong security mechanisms to prevent unauthorized access, data breaches, and cyber threats.

Storage security focuses on protecting data at rest, ensuring that data remains confidential, intact, and available while being stored on various media such as hard drives (HDDs), solid-state drives (SSDs), and network-attached storage (NAS) systems.

Encryption plays a key role in securing data by converting readable data into an encoded format, which can only be decrypted using an authorized key. This ensures that even if an attacker gains access to the storage medium, the data remains unreadable without the proper decryption credentials.

Threats to Data Storage Security

Several factors pose threats to stored data, including physical theft, cyber-attacks, **malware, and insider threats**. The most common storage security threats include:

1. **Unauthorized Access:** Unprotected storage devices can be accessed by **hackers, rogue employees, or malicious insiders.**
2. **Data Breaches:** Cybercriminals exploit vulnerabilities to steal sensitive information such as financial records, personal identification details, and intellectual property.
3. **Ransomware Attacks:** Malicious software encrypts user data and demands a ransom for decryption keys.
4. **Data Corruption and Loss:** Hardware failures, software errors, or human mistakes can cause irreversible data loss.
5. **Physical Theft of Storage Devices:** If storage devices are lost or stolen, the stored data may be exposed without adequate security measures.

Types of Storage Encryption

Encryption ensures that stored data remains secure even if an unauthorized party gains access to the storage medium. The two main types of storage encryption are hardware-based encryption and software-based encryption.

1. Hardware-Based Encryption

- Performed at the hardware level within the storage device.
- It uses **self-encrypting drives (SEDs)**, where encryption and decryption occur automatically.
- Offers higher performance and lower CPU overhead compared to software encryption.
- Used in enterprise servers, banking institutions, and government agencies.

Example

- **Trusted Platform Module (TPM):** A secure chip integrated into modern motherboards that stores encryption keys.
- **AES-256 Encryption on SSDs:** Ensures strong security for solid-state drives used in enterprise environments.

2. Software-Based Encryption

- Performed by encryption programs such as BitLocker (Windows), FileVault (macOS), and VeraCrypt (cross-platform).
- It is more flexible as it can be applied to specific files, folders, or entire drives.
- It may have higher CPU overhead since encryption processes run through software.
- Suitable for personal users, small businesses, and cloud-based storage solutions.

Example

- **BitLocker Drive Encryption:** Integrated into Windows OS for encrypting entire storage volumes.
- **VeraCrypt:** Open-source encryption software for securing individual files and partitions.

Data Security Best Practices for Storage

To prevent unauthorized access and ensure data integrity, organizations and individuals must adopt the following data security best practices:

1. Implement Multi-Factor Authentication (MF(a)

- Multiple authentication steps (e.g., password + biometric verification) are required to access storage systems.
- Ensures that even if one authentication factor is compromised, unauthorized access is prevented.

2. Regular Data Backups and Redundancy

- Maintain offline backups to recover from cyberattacks, hardware failures, or accidental deletions.
- Use RAID storage solutions and cloud backups to ensure redundancy.
- Follow the 3-2-1 Backup Rule:
  - 3 copies of data (1 primary, 2 backups).
  - 2 different storage media (HDD, SSD, cloud, etc.).
  - 1 offsite backup for disaster recovery.

3. Secure Cloud Storage with End-to-End Encryption

- Use zero-trust cloud storage providers that offer end-to-end encryption.
- Ensure data is encrypted before uploading to the cloud.
- Enable two-factor authentication (2F(a) for cloud storage accounts.

4. Data Masking and Tokenization

- Data masking replaces sensitive information with placeholders while maintaining usability.
- Tokenization replaces sensitive data with unique tokens, reducing the risk of exposure to data breaches.
- Used in financial transactions, healthcare records, and online payment gateways.

5. Secure Physical Storage Media

- Store external hard drives, USB flash drives, and SSDs in locked cabinets or safes.
- Use tamper-proof security features such as hardware locks and biometric access.
- Properly dispose of old storage devices by securely erasing or physically destroying them.

Regulatory Compliance for Data Storage Security

Various international regulations mandate strict security practices for storing personal and enterprise data. Some key compliance frameworks include:

Table 3.12 outlines key data security compliance standards and their descriptions, emphasizing the importance of regulatory frameworks in protecting sensitive information. GDPR enforces strict data protection laws in the EU. At the same time, HIPAA mandates secure handling of patient health records in the U.S. PCI DSS ensures the safe storage of financial and credit card data, and FISMA establishes data security regulations for U.S. federal agencies. These standards are critical for maintaining data integrity, security, and regulatory compliance across various industries.

Table 3.12: *Key Data Security Compliance Standards and Their Descriptions*

Compliance Standard	Description
General Data Protection Regulation (GDPR)	EU law requires strict data protection and encryption for personal information.
Health Insurance Portability and Accountability Act (HIPA(a)	Mandates encryption for patient health records in the U.S. healthcare sector.
Payment Card Industry Data Security Standard (PCI DSS)	Requires secure storage of financial data and credit card transactions.
Federal Information Security Management Act (FISM(a)	U.S. regulation governing data security for federal agencies.

Organizations handling sensitive data must ensure compliance with these security standards to prevent legal consequences and protect user information.

Conclusion

Storage security and encryption are essential to protect sensitive data from unauthorized access, cyber threats, and physical theft. Implementing strong encryption mechanisms, secure authentication methods, and data redundancy strategies ensures long-term data integrity and compliance with security regulations.

The following section will focus on emerging storage technologies, highlighting advancements in quantum storage, DNA data storage, and AI-driven storage management.

Interesting Facts

- **Invisible Armor:** Encryption turns readable data into unintelligible code, acting like a digital armour that protects our most sensitive information from unauthorized access.
- **Ubiquitous Security:** From personal smartphones to enterprise data centres, encryption is used everywhere—from securing emails and chats to protecting financial transactions.
- **Hardware vs. Software:** While hardware-based encryption offers high performance with minimal CPU overhead, software-based solutions provide flexibility and can be tailored to encrypt specific files, folders, or entire drives.

Video Resources

- **Overview Videos:** Search for "Introduction to Storage Security and Encryption" on YouTube to find animated explanations of how encryption works and why it is essential.
- **Tutorials:** Look for step-by-step guides such as "How to Encrypt Your Hard Drive with BitLocker" or "Using VeraCrypt for Secure File Encryption."
- **Expert Talks:** Channels like *Security Now* and *The PC Security Channel* often feature discussions on data breaches, encryption standards (like AES-256), and emerging trends in storage security.

Use of ICT

- **Data Protection Tools:** ICT systems employ encryption software (e.g., BitLocker, FileVault, VeraCrypt) to secure data at rest, while hardware encryption modules (like TPMs) ensure that key management is robust.
- **Remote Monitoring and Management:** ICT solutions integrate secure remote access and monitoring tools, allowing IT teams to track unauthorized access attempts and manage encryption policies across distributed networks.
- **Compliance Automation:** Automated systems use encryption combined with access controls and audit trails to help organizations meet regulatory standards like GDPR, HIPAA, and PCI DSS.

Applications (Real Life/Industrial)

- **Personal Devices:** Smartphones, laptops, and tablets use encryption to secure sensitive personal data, from photos to banking information.
- **Enterprise Environments:** Data centres and cloud storage services use end-to-end encryption to protect vast amounts of corporate data and customer records, ensuring compliance and trust.
- **Industrial Systems:** Critical infrastructure—such as energy grids and manufacturing control systems—rely on encrypted communications and storage to prevent cyberattacks that could disrupt essential services.
- **Financial Institutions:** Banks and payment processors use encryption to secure transactions, safeguard customer data, and prevent fraud.

Case Study (Environmental/Sustainability/Social/Ethical Issues)

Context

A multinational healthcare organization needed to protect sensitive patient data while also addressing concerns about energy consumption and electronic waste in its data centres.

Scenario

- **Challenge:** With rising cyber threats and stringent regulations like HIPAA and GDPR, the organization faced the dual challenge of ensuring robust data encryption and reducing the environmental impact of its IT infrastructure.

- **Solution**
  - **Hardware-Based Encryption:** The organization upgraded its storage devices to self-encrypting drives (SEDs) that utilize AES-256 encryption, reducing CPU overhead and improving energy efficiency.
  - **Secure Cloud Storage:** Data was encrypted end-to-end before being transmitted to the cloud, ensuring that patient records remained confidential even if intercepted.
  - **Sustainability Measures:** By consolidating data centres and implementing energy-efficient cooling and power systems, the organization reduced its carbon footprint and extended the lifespan of its storage devices.
- **Impact**
  - Enhanced data security and regulatory compliance.
  - Lower energy consumption and reduced electronic waste.
  - Strengthened public trust through responsible, ethical IT practices.

Discussion Points

- How do encryption and energy-efficient hardware work together to reduce the environmental impact of data centres?
- What are the ethical responsibilities of organizations in protecting personal data while also minimizing their carbon footprint?
- Can advancements in green technology further enhance data security without compromising performance?

Create Inquisitiveness and Curiosity

- **Speculative Inquiry:** Imagine a future where quantum computers break current encryption standards. How might new encryption methods evolve to protect data in that era?
- **Design Challenge:** If we were to design a secure storage system for a remote research station in an extreme environment, what encryption protocols and physical security measures would we prioritize?
- **Debate Prompt:** Should companies be legally required to use the strongest available encryption methods, even if it might slow down system performance? What are the trade-offs?
- **Innovation Brainstorm:** Can we devise a hybrid encryption approach that seamlessly integrates both hardware and software methods to optimize security and energy efficiency?

Solved Problems (With Increasing Difficulty Level)

Problem 1 (Basic)

Question

What is the primary purpose of encryption in storage security?

Solution

Encryption converts data into an unreadable format so that even if unauthorized users gain access to the storage device, they cannot decipher the information without the correct decryption key.

Problem 2 (Intermediate)

Question

Compare hardware-based encryption with software-based encryption in terms of performance and flexibility.

Solution

- **Hardware-Based Encryption:**
  - Performed at the device level (e.g., self-encrypting drives).
  - Offers high performance with minimal CPU overhead.
  - Ideal for enterprise systems where speed is crucial.
- **Software-Based Encryption:**
  - Performed by applications (e.g., BitLocker, VeraCrypt).
  - It provides greater flexibility by allowing the selective encryption of files or partitions.
  - It may incur higher CPU overhead, making it better suited for personal or small business use.

Problem 3 (Advanced)

Question

Explain how multi-factor authentication (MF(a) enhances storage security, particularly in environments that use encryption.

Solution

Multi-factor authentication (MF(a) requires users to provide two or more verification factors (e.g., a password plus biometric dat(a) before accessing encrypted data. This added layer of security ensures that even if encryption keys or passwords are compromised, unauthorized access is still prevented. MFA reduces the risk of data breaches by making it significantly harder for attackers to bypass multiple authentication barriers.

Problem 4 (Challenging)

Question

A company needs to secure its sensitive customer data stored on both local servers and in the cloud. Propose a comprehensive security strategy that incorporates encryption, MFA, and redundancy. Justify your approach.

Solution

- **A comprehensive strategy could include:**
  - **End-to-End Encryption:** Encrypt data before it leaves the local servers using hardware-based encryption for local storage and software-based encryption

for specific data sets. This ensures that data remains secure both at rest and during transmission.

- **Multi-Factor Authentication (MF(a):** Implement MFA for accessing both local systems and cloud storage to provide additional verification, significantly reducing the risk of unauthorized access.
- **Data Redundancy and Backup:** Utilize RAID configurations locally to ensure data is mirrored or striped with parity (such as RAID 5 or RAID 10) and integrate regular, encrypted cloud backups following the 3-2-1 backup rule. This guarantees data availability and quick recovery in case of hardware failures or cyberattacks.

Justification

- **Encryption:** Protects data confidentiality even if storage devices are compromised.
- **MFA:** Adds a critical security layer that safeguards against password breaches.
- **Redundancy:** Ensures that data loss is minimized through both local and cloud backups, maintaining business continuity and regulatory compliance.

This strategy balances high-level security, operational efficiency, and compliance with industry regulations while mitigating risks associated with data breaches and hardware failures.

3.5 EMERGING STORAGE TECHNOLOGIES

Introduction to Emerging Storage Technologies

With the exponential growth of digital data, traditional storage solutions such as hard disk drives (HDDs) and solid-state drives (SSDs) are being pushed to their limits. The demand for higher capacity, faster speeds, and improved efficiency has led to the development of next-generation storage technologies that integrate quantum storage, DNA data storage, AI-enhanced storage management, and persistent memory.

Emerging storage technologies aim to address challenges related to data density, security, energy consumption, and reliability, making them suitable for big data, artificial intelligence (AI), high-performance computing (HP(c), and cloud infrastructure.

Quantum Storage

Overview

Quantum storage is a revolutionary concept that leverages the principles of quantum mechanics to store and retrieve information at unprecedented speeds and capacities. Unlike classical storage devices that store data in binary (0s and 1s), quantum storage utilizes quantum bits (qubits), which can exist in multiple states simultaneously due to **superposition and entanglement**.

Key Features of Quantum Storage

- **Ultra-Fast Data Processing:** Quantum storage enables instant data retrieval through **quantum entanglement**.
- **Massive Data Density:** This can store significantly more information compared to conventional storage mediums.

- **Unbreakable Security:** Uses quantum cryptography to prevent unauthorized access and data breaches.

Example

- IBM and Google are developing **quantum computing storage models** that promise speeds far beyond today's fastest SSDs.

Figure 28 illustrates the Quantum Storage Concept and Qubit Representation, showcasing how quantum information is stored, manipulated, and retrieved in quantum computing systems.

Quantum storage relies on qubits (quantum bits), which differ from classical bits by existing in a state of superposition, meaning they can represent both 0 and 1 simultaneously. The process begins with writing quantum information into a quantum medium, where interactions between quantum particles, such as electron spins or superconducting circuits, store the data. Later, the stored qubits are read back while maintaining quantum coherence, ensuring reliable data retrieval.

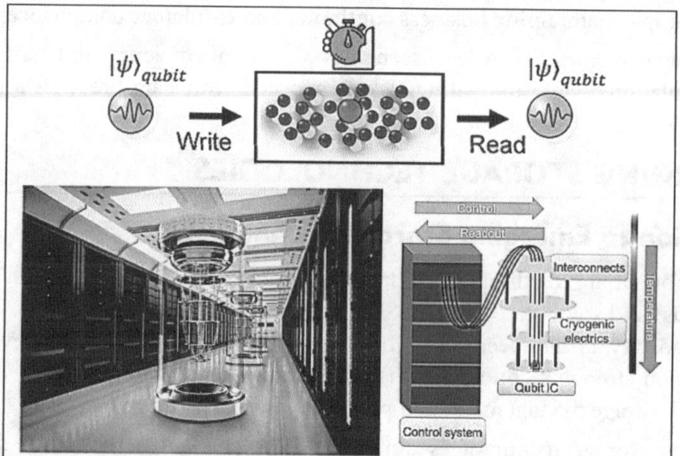

Figure 3.8: Quantum Storage Concept and Qubit Representation

The diagram also highlights a quantum computing data centre, showcasing the cryogenic cooling systems required to maintain qubit stability at extremely low temperatures. A detailed schematic further explains the control system, interconnects, cryogenic electrics, and qubit IC (Integrated Circuit), all crucial for processing quantum information.

This concept represents the foundation of next-generation computing, enabling breakthroughs in encryption, AI, scientific simulations, and cloud-based quantum storage, where massive parallelism and ultra-fast computations redefine traditional data processing.

DNA Data Storage

Overview

DNA data storage is an innovative method that encodes digital data into synthetic DNA strands. Since DNA molecules can store vast amounts of information in a highly compact and durable form, researchers are exploring it as a potential replacement for conventional storage devices.

Key Features of DNA Storage

- **Extraordinary Data Density:** 1 gram of DNA can theoretically store 215 petabytes (P(b) of data.
- **Extreme Longevity:** DNA can last for thousands of years without degradation.
- **Eco-Friendly and Low Energy Consumption:** This does not require continuous power for data retention.

Example

- Microsoft and the University of Washington have successfully demonstrated DNA-based storage systems, encoding and retrieving large datasets.

Figure 29 illustrates the DNA Data Encoding and Retrieval Process, demonstrating how digital information can be stored in DNA molecules for ultra-dense, long-term archival storage.

The process begins with encoding, where binary data (0s and 1s) from a digital file is converted into a DNA sequence consisting of nucleotide bases (A, T, C, G). These sequences are then synthesized into actual DNA molecules and stored in specialized containers, such as test tubes or microfluidic chips, where they remain stable for extended periods.

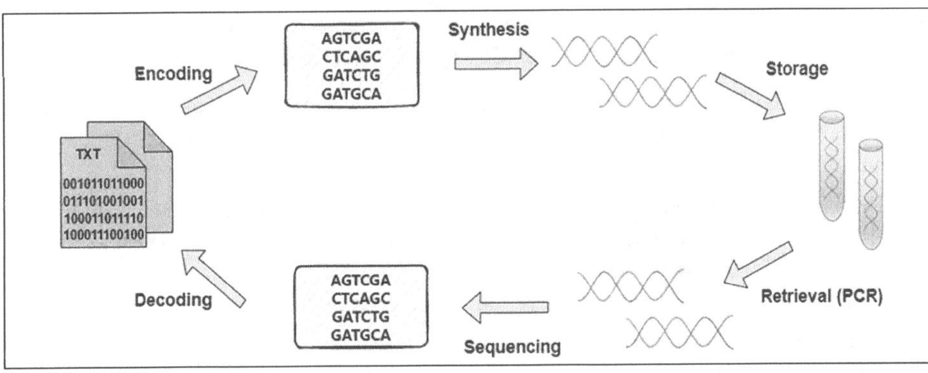

***Figure 3.9:** DNA Data Encoding and Retrieval Process*

To retrieve the stored data, a Polymerase Chain Reaction (PCR) is used to amplify the required DNA sequences, followed by DNA sequencing, which reads the stored nucleotide data. The final step involves decoding, where the DNA sequence is translated back into its original binary format, reconstructing the digital file.

This revolutionary storage method offers unmatched data density, stability, and longevity, making DNA storage a promising solution for archiving vast amounts of digital information, with potential applications in genomics, cloud storage, and future-proof data preservation.

AI-Driven Storage Management

Overview

Artificial Intelligence (AI) is transforming storage management by automating data optimization, predictive analytics, and workload balancing. AI-driven storage solutions analyze storage usage patterns to enhance performance, efficiency, and reliability.

Key Features of AI-Driven Storage

- **Predictive Failure Analysis:** AI detects potential hardware failures before they occur, preventing data loss.
- **Automated Data Tiering:** AI moves frequently accessed data to high-speed storage while archiving less-used data to slower, cost-effective storage.
- **Self-Healing Storage Systems:** AI-based solutions can automatically correct corrupted data and optimize redundancy.

Example

- Google Cloud and Amazon AWS implement AI-powered storage optimization to reduce latency and maximize resource efficiency.

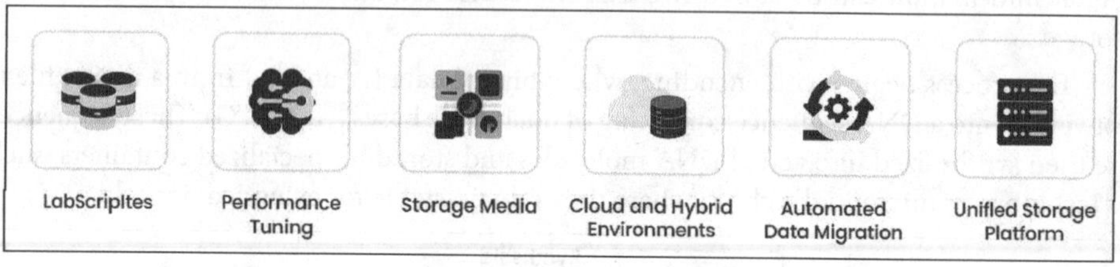

Figure 3.10: *AI-Driven Storage Optimization Workflow*

Figure 3.10 illustrates the DNA Data Encoding and Retrieval Process, demonstrating how digital information can be stored in DNA molecules for ultra-dense, long-term archival storage.

The process begins with encoding, where binary data (0s and 1s) from a digital file is converted into a DNA sequence consisting of nucleotide bases (A, T, C, G). These sequences are then synthesized into actual DNA molecules and stored in specialized containers, such as test tubes or microfluidic chips, where they remain stable for extended periods.

To retrieve the stored data, a Polymerase Chain Reaction (PCR) is used to amplify the required DNA sequences, followed by DNA sequencing, which reads the stored nucleotide data. The final step involves decoding, where the DNA sequence is translated back into its original binary format, reconstructing the digital file.

This revolutionary storage method offers unmatched data density, stability, and longevity, making DNA storage a promising solution for archiving vast amounts of digital information, with potential applications in genomics, cloud storage, and future-proof data preservation.

Persistent Memory (PMEM)

Overview

Persistent Memory (PMEM) is a hybrid storage solution that combines the speed of DRAM with the non-volatility of SSDs. It enables faster data access, making it ideal for high-performance computing (HP(c), real-time analytics, and database acceleration.

Key Features of PMEM

- **Lower Latency than SSDs:** Enables near-instantaneous data retrieval.
- **Data Persistence:** Unlike DRAM, PMEM retains data even after power loss.

- **High-Speed Database Processing:** Used in applications requiring real-time data insights.

Example

- Intel Optane Persistent Memory significantly improves server performance and database efficiency.

Holographic Storage

Overview

Holographic storage records data in three-dimensional light patterns, allowing multiple layers of data to be stored in the same physical space. This technology promises high-speed data access with immense storage capacity.

Key Features of Holographic Storage

- **Multi-Layer Storage Capability:** Can store several terabytes of data per disc.
- **Longer Lifespan:** More durable than conventional optical storage.
- **High-Speed Data Transfer:** Enables rapid read and write operations.

Example

- GE and IBM are researching **holographic storage discs** for next-generation archival solutions.

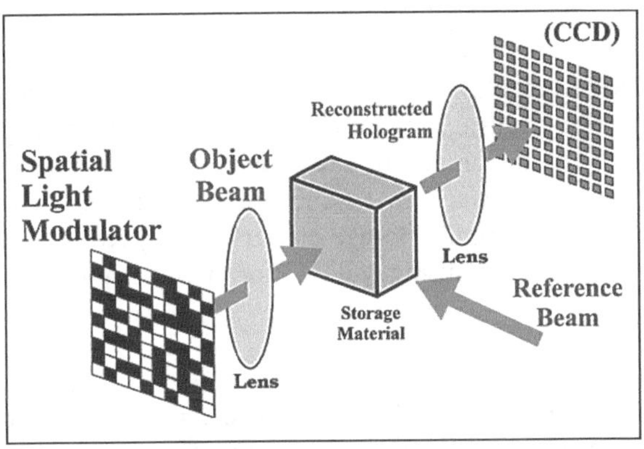

Figure 3.11: *Holographic Storage Mechanism*

Figure 3.11 illustrates the Holographic Storage Mechanism, a next-generation data storage technology that utilizes laser-based holography to encode and retrieve information.

The process begins with a Spatial Light Modulator (SLM), which encodes digital data into a 2D light pattern. This pattern is then passed through a lens, forming an object beam that interacts with the storage material. Simultaneously, a reference beam is directed toward the storage medium, creating an interference pattern that records the data as a hologram.

For retrieval, the reference beam is projected back onto the storage material, reconstructing the stored hologram. A lens then focuses the reconstructed data onto a CCD (Charge-Coupled Device) sensor, which converts the optical hologram back into digital information.

Holographic storage offers high-density data capacity, parallel data access, and long-term stability, making it a promising technology for large-scale archival storage, scientific research, and high-speed data applications.

Table 3.13: Comparison of Emerging Storage Technologies

Storage Technology	Speed	Data Density	Longevity	Use Cases
Quantum Storage	Ultra-Fast	Extremely High	Experimental	Quantum Computing, AI Processing
DNA Storage	Slow (Current Tech)	215 PB per gram	Thousands of Years	Long-Term Archival, Bioinformatics
AI-Driven Storage	Variable	Adaptive	Continuous Improvement	Cloud Computing, Data Centers
Persistent Memory (PMEM)	Faster than SSDs	High	Retains Data After Power Loss	HPC, Database Acceleration
Holographic Storage	High	High	50+ Years	Archival, High-Speed Data Retrieval

Table 3.13 compares emerging storage technologies based on speed, data density, longevity, and primary use cases. Quantum storage offers ultra-fast speeds and is ideal for AI processing and quantum computing.

In contrast, DNA storage provides unparalleled data density and longevity, making it suitable for long-term archival applications. AI-driven storage adapts dynamically to workloads, benefiting cloud computing and data centres, whereas persistent memory (PMEM) bridges the gap between RAM and SSDs, enhancing database performance and HPC applications. Holographic storage delivers high-speed data retrieval with long-term reliability, making it a promising solution for archival storage and large-scale data applications.

Conclusion

Emerging storage technologies hold the potential to revolutionize data storage, offering solutions that are faster, denser, and more energy-efficient than current technologies. While some innovations, like AI-driven storage and persistent memory, are already being integrated into enterprise solutions, others, like quantum storage and DNA storage, are still in the experimental phase. Understanding these emerging technologies will help organizations future-proof their data infrastructure and prepare for the next-generation computing landscape.

The following section will summarize key concepts of storage technologies and include exercises to reinforce learning.

Interesting Facts

- **Beyond Bits:** Emerging storage technologies are pushing the boundaries of data storage by moving beyond traditional binary systems. Quantum storage and DNA storage use principles of quantum mechanics and biology to encode information, opening up revolutionary possibilities.

- **Unprecedented Density:** For example, 1 gram of DNA could theoretically store up to 215 petabytes of data—a storage density that far surpasses conventional HDDs and SSDs.
- **AI at the Helm:** AI-driven storage management systems are learning from data usage patterns to optimize performance and predict failures, effectively creating self-healing data centres.

Video Resources

- **Overview Videos:** Search for "Emerging Storage Technologies Explained" or "Future of Data Storage" on YouTube to find animated and expert-led discussions on quantum storage, DNA storage, and more.
- **Tutorials & Demos:** Look for content like "How AI is Revolutionizing Storage Management" or "Understanding Persistent Memory (PMEM)" for practical demonstrations and technical breakdowns.
- **Expert Panels:** Channels such as *IEEE Spectrum* and *TechLinked* often host panels and interviews discussing the latest innovations in storage technology and their future implications.

Use of ICT

- **Data-Driven Insights:** ICT systems now leverage AI algorithms to manage and optimize emerging storage technologies, enabling real-time data analytics and predictive maintenance.
- **Virtual Prototyping:** Advanced simulation tools help researchers model quantum and holographic storage systems before physical prototypes are built, reducing development time and costs.
- **Enhanced Security & Efficiency:** Emerging storage technologies incorporate state-of-the-art encryption and energy-efficient designs, which are managed through centralized ICT platforms to ensure data integrity and sustainability.

Applications (Real Life/Industrial)

- **High-Performance Computing (HP(c):** Persistent memory (PMEM) and AI-driven storage solutions accelerate data processing and real-time analytics in scientific research and financial modelling.
- **Cloud Infrastructure:** AI-enhanced storage management systems optimize resource allocation in cloud data centres, ensuring rapid data access and high availability for users worldwide.
- **Long-Term Archival:** DNA storage and holographic storage offer ultra-dense, long-lasting solutions for archival purposes, ideal for institutions like national libraries and research organizations.
- **Quantum Computing:** Quantum storage is being explored for next-generation computing, where ultra-fast data processing is essential for complex AI and machine learning tasks.

Case Study (Environmental/Sustainability/Social/Ethical Issues)

Context

A global research institute sought to overhaul its data storage infrastructure to handle explosive data growth while minimizing environmental impact and ensuring long-term data preservation.

Scenario

- **Challenge:** Traditional storage systems were reaching their limits in terms of capacity, energy consumption, and e-waste generation. The institute needed a solution that was both future-proof and sustainable.
- **Solution:**
  - **Hybrid Implementation:** The institute piloted a hybrid storage system combining AI-driven storage management with persistent memory (PMEM) for high-speed operations and holographic storage for archival purposes.
  - **Energy Efficiency:** By incorporating technologies like PMEM and holographic storage, the institute reduced energy usage, as these systems require less power than conventional SSDs/HDDs.
  - **Sustainability Focus:** They also initiated a recycling program for outdated hardware and invested in research on DNA data storage, which promises long-term durability without continuous power consumption.
- **Impact**
  - The new system achieved a significant reduction in energy consumption and e-waste.
  - Data retrieval times improved dramatically, supporting advanced research projects.
  - The institute became a model for sustainable IT practices, influencing policies on green computing.

Discussion Points

- How can emerging storage technologies contribute to reducing the carbon footprint of large data centres?
- What ethical considerations arise when transitioning to experimental storage methods like DNA storage?
- In what ways can research institutions take charge of adopting sustainable storage solutions globally?

Create Inquisitiveness and Curiosity

- **Future Vision:** How might the integration of quantum storage with AI-driven management redefine our approach to big data and machine learning in the next decade?
- **Design Challenge:** Imagine designing a storage system for an interplanetary mission. What emerging storage technologies will we choose, and how will we address challenges like radiation and extreme temperatures?

- **Debate:** Should the tech industry prioritize the rapid adoption of emerging storage technologies over the risks of unproven performance and scalability? What factors should influence this decision?
- **Innovation Brainstorm:** Can we conceive a new storage concept that combines elements of holographic storage and DNA storage? What potential benefits and challenges could such a hybrid system present?

Solved Problems (With Increasing Difficulty Level)

Problem 1 (Basic)

Question

What is one key advantage of DNA data storage compared to traditional HDDs?

Solution

DNA data storage offers extraordinary data density; theoretically, 1 gram of DNA can store up to 215 petabytes of data, far exceeding the storage capacity of conventional HDDs.

Problem 2 (Intermediate)

Question

Explain how AI-driven storage management improves the performance and reliability of modern data centres.

Solution

AI-driven storage management analyzes data usage patterns to automatically optimize data placement, predict hardware failures, and perform self-healing corrections. This leads to reduced latency, improved performance, and enhanced fault tolerance in data centres.

Problem 3 (Advanced

Question

Compare persistent memory (PMEM) with traditional SSDs in terms of speed and data persistence. What advantages does PMEM offer for high-performance computing?

Solution

Persistent memory (PMEM) combines the speed of DRAM with the non-volatility of SSDs. It offers lower latency than SSDs, ensuring near-instantaneous data retrieval, and retains data even after power loss. This makes PMEM ideal for high-performance computing applications that require rapid access to large datasets and real-time data processing.

Problem 4 (Challenging)

Question

A cloud service provider aims to integrate emerging storage technologies to enhance service efficiency and reduce environmental impact. Propose a hybrid storage strategy that combines at least two emerging technologies. Explain our choice and address potential trade-offs.

Solution

A viable hybrid strategy could involve:

- **AI-Driven Storage Management Combined with Persistent Memory (PMEM):**
  - **Implementation:** Use PMEM for high-speed data processing and real-time analytics, managed by AI algorithms, to dynamically optimize workload distribution and predict failures.
  - **Advantages:** This setup enhances performance for critical applications while reducing energy consumption due to the low latency and power efficiency of PMEM.
- **Integration of Holographic Storage for Archival:**
  - **Implementation:** Deploy holographic storage systems for long-term, high-capacity archival of less frequently accessed data.
  - **Advantages:** Holographic storage offers multi-layer data recording with a long lifespan (50+ years) and high-speed data transfer for retrieval.
- **Trade-Offs:**
  - **Complexity:** Integrating different technologies requires sophisticated management software and increased initial capital investment.
  - **Performance Balance:** While PMEM provides rapid access, holographic storage may have slower write speeds; hence, careful data tiering is necessary to ensure optimal performance.

This hybrid approach balances speed, capacity, energy efficiency, and environmental sustainability, making it ideal for a cloud service provider aiming to deliver high-performance services while reducing its carbon footprint.

SUMMARY

This unit covered various storage technologies, modern data interfaces, RAID configurations, security measures, and emerging innovations. The key topics discussed include:

- **Types of Storage Technologies:** Understanding primary, secondary, and tertiary storage, including HDDs, SSDs, hybrid drives, and cloud storage.
- **Modern Data Interfaces:** Overview of SATA, NVMe, PCIe, USB, and Thunderbolt, as well as their speeds and use cases.
- **RAID (Redundant Array of Independent Disks):** Explanation of RAID 0, RAID 1, RAID 5, RAID 6, and RAID 10, focusing on performance and fault tolerance.
- **Storage Security and Encryption:** Protecting data using hardware-based and software-based encryption, along with best security practices.
- **Emerging Storage Technologies:** Innovations such as quantum storage, DNA data storage, AI-driven storage, persistent memory, and holographic storage.

EXERCISES

1. Subjective Questions (Conceptual and Analytical)

1. Explain the differences between HDDs and SSDs in terms of performance, durability, and power consumption.

2. Describe the advantages and limitations of NVMe over SATA SSDs.
3. What are the key benefits of RAID 10 over RAID 5? Discuss the fault tolerance mechanisms in both.
4. How does AI-driven storage management improve efficiency in data centres?
5. What are the security risks associated with cloud storage, and how can they be mitigated?
6. Explain how quantum storage differs from traditional storage devices.
7. Discuss the potential of DNA data storage and its advantages over magnetic storage.
8. What role does persistent memory (PMEM) play in database acceleration?
9. Compare and contrast holographic storage and optical disc storage.
10. Describe the challenges of integrating emerging storage technologies into current computing infrastructures.

2. Objective Questions (Multiple-Choice and True/False)

Multiple-choice questions (MCQs)

1. Which storage interface offers the highest data transfer speeds?
   (a) SATA 3.0 (b) NVMe
   (c) USB 3.1 (d) Thunderbolt
2. RAID 1 is best suited for:
   (a) High-speed data transfers (b) Data mirroring and redundancy
   (c) Striping without redundancy (d) Temporary caching
3. Which encryption method operates at the hardware level?
   (a) AES-256 Software Encryption (b) BitLocker
   (c) TPM (Trusted Platform Module) (d) VeraCrypt
4. DNA storage is primarily used for:
   (a) High-speed computing (b) Long-term archival data storage
   (c) Real-time analytics (d) Cloud-based storage
5. AI-driven storage solutions help in:
   (a) Reducing energy consumption (b) Predicting drive failures
   (c) Optimizing data tiering (d) All of the above

True/False Questions

1. NVMe storage operates through SATA ports. *(True/False)*
2. RAID 6 can tolerate two drive failures while maintaining data integrity. *(True/False)*
3. Persistent memory (PMEM) loses data when power is lost. *(True/False)*
4. Holographic storage uses quantum mechanics to store data. *(True/False)*
5. Cloud storage with **end-to-end encryption** ensures that only the user can access their data. *(True/False)*

TEACHER'S KNOW MORE

For educators and advanced learners, additional insights and references include:

- **Storage Virtualization:** How virtual storage solutions enhance enterprise cloud computing.
- **Future of AI in Storage Management:** How AI will transform predictive maintenance, workload balancing, and real-time optimization.
- **Regulatory Compliance:** Understanding GDPR, HIPAA, and PCI DSS in secure storage implementation.
- **Hands-on Labs for RAID Configurations:** Setting up RAID in Windows, Linux, and enterprise storage servers.
- **Next-Generation Storage Research:** Exploration of neuromorphic storage and molecular memory technologies.

4

UNIT

MEMORY MANAGEMENT AND OPTIMIZATION

RATIONALE

Modern computer systems rely heavily on I/O peripherals and efficient bus architectures to facilitate communication between the central processor and external devices. This unit is designed to provide a deep understanding of the various input/output devices, the differences between parallel and serial communication, and the evolution of bus standards from legacy interfaces to modern high-speed connections. By examining video and audio peripherals alongside their integration with bus architectures, students will develop the skills to design and troubleshoot systems that ensure fast, reliable data transfer and enhance human-computer interaction.

Key learning benefits include:

- **Enhanced System Integration:** Understand how different peripheral devices interact with the CPU and memory via various bus architectures.
- **Technological Evolution:** Learn about the historical progression from ISA to PCIe, which underscores the rapid evolution in data transfer methods.
- **Practical Application:** Apply theoretical concepts to real-world scenarios, including setting up and optimizing I/O systems for various computing environments.
- **Innovation and Future Trends:** Explore emerging trends in display and audio technologies, preparing students for advanced research and professional practice in systems design.

OUTCOMES

By the end of this unit, students will be able to:

- **Define and Categorize I/O Peripherals:**
  - Understand the roles of input, output, and storage devices in computing.
  - Explain how peripheral devices contribute to overall system performance.
- **Differentiate Communication Protocols:**
  - Distinguish between parallel and serial communication, and identify common standards (e.g., RS-232, RS-485, USB, Thunderbolt).
  - Interpret timing diagrams and data transfer mechanisms.
- **Analyze Bus Architectures:**
  - Compare legacy and modern bus architectures (ISA, PCI, AGP, PCIe) in terms of speed, efficiency, and application.
  - Understand synchronous versus asynchronous communication methods.
- **Evaluate Video and Audio Peripherals:**
  - Describe various video adapters (VGA, HDMI, DisplayPort, DVI) and audio peripherals (sound cards, speakers).
  - Discuss the impact of human-computer interaction (HCI) on peripheral design and the latest trends in display and sound technologies.

- **Apply Knowledge to Practical Scenarios:**
  - Recommend suitable I/O configurations for specific applications.
  - Develop troubleshooting strategies for bus-related and peripheral issues.

4.1 INTRODUCTION TO MEMORY MANAGEMENT

Overview of Memory Management

Memory management is a crucial aspect of modern computing that ensures efficient allocation, utilization, and protection of system memory resources. Effective memory management optimizes system performance, prevents memory leaks, and enables multitasking environments to function smoothly.

Computers use a combination of primary memory (RAM), secondary memory (HDD/SS(d), and cache memory to process data efficiently. The operating system (OS) is responsible for managing memory allocation and ensuring that processes receive the necessary memory resources while preventing conflicts.

Types of Memory in Computing

Memory in a computer system is broadly classified into volatile and non-volatile memory:

1. Volatile Memory

- **Random Access Memory (RAM):** Temporary storage that allows fast data access but loses its content when power is turned off.
- **Cache Memory:** A small, high-speed memory unit within the CPU that stores frequently accessed data.
- **Registers:** The fastest memory located inside the CPU, used for executing instructions.

2. Non-Volatile Memory

- **Read-Only Memory (ROM):** Stores firmware and system boot instructions.
- **Flash Memory:** Used in SSDs and USB drives for permanent data storage.
- **Hard Disk Drives (HDDs) and Solid-State Drives (SSDs):** Used for long-term data storage.

Memory Hierarchy in Computer Architecture

The memory hierarchy in computing is structured based on speed, cost, and proximity to the CPU:

Table 4.2 presents the hierarchy of memory types, comparing their speed, size, and primary use cases. Registers are the fastest and smallest, directly storing CPU instructions for immediate execution. Cache memory provides quick access to frequently used data, improving processor efficiency.

RAM serves as volatile storage for active processes, while SSDs offer fast, non-volatile storage for permanent data. HDDs, though the slowest, provide the largest storage capacity, making them ideal for long-term mass storage and backups.

Table 4.2: Hierarchy of Memory Types: Speed, Size, and Use Cases

Memory Type	Speed	Size	Use Case
Registers	Fastest	Smallest	Stores CPU instructions
Cache Memory	Very Fast	Small	Stores frequently accessed data
RAM	Fast	Medium	Stores active processes
SSD	Moderate	Large	Permanent storage
HDD	Slowest	Largest	Mass storage

Memory Management Techniques

The operating system employs different memory management techniques to optimize resource usage and prevent fragmentation and memory leaks:

1. Contiguous Memory Allocation

- Assign a single continuous block of memory to each process.
- Simple but suffers from external fragmentation.

2. Paging

- Divides memory into fixed-size blocks called pages, eliminating external fragmentation.
- Allows non-contiguous memory allocation, improving efficiency.

3. Segmentation

- Divides memory based on logical divisions such as functions, data, and stack segments.
- It is more flexible than paging but may cause internal fragmentation.

4. Virtual Memory

- It uses disk space as an extension of RAM, allowing systems to handle larger applications than physical memory allows.
- It enables multitasking but can be slower due to disk swapping.

Role of Memory Optimization in System Performance

Effective memory management enhances processing speed, stability, and overall system performance. Key optimization techniques include:

- **Memory Compression:** Reducing the size of stored data to optimize RAM usage.
- **Garbage Collection:** Automatically deallocating unused memory in programming environments like Java and Python.
- **Disk Caching:** Storing frequently accessed files in faster storage media to **reduce load times**.
- **Defragmentation:** Reorganizing data on HDDs to improve read/write speeds.

Example: *Windows and Linux use virtual memory (swap space) to manage memory efficiently when RAM is fully utilized.*

Conclusion

Memory management plays a vital role in enhancing computing performance, reducing bottlenecks, and ensuring efficient resource allocation. Modern operating systems use paging, segmentation, and virtual memory techniques to handle memory efficiently.

The following section will explore Memory Allocation Strategies, detailing how operating systems allocate memory to processes and optimize system performance.

4.2 MEMORY ALLOCATION STRATEGIES

Introduction to Memory Allocation

Memory allocation refers to the process by which the operating system (OS) assigns memory blocks to various processes and applications. Efficient memory allocation ensures optimal system performance, minimizes fragmentation, and prevents memory leaks.

There Are Two Primary Types Of Memory Allocation:

- **Static Memory Allocation:** Memory is assigned at compile-time and remains fixed.
- **Dynamic Memory Allocation:** Memory is assigned at runtime and can change based on program needs.

Modern operating systems use different allocation techniques to manage memory efficiently and prevent system slowdowns due to fragmentation or excessive memory usage.

Types of Memory Allocation Strategies

1. Single-Partition Allocation

- The entire memory is allocated to a single process.
- Used in early computing systems but inefficient for multitasking.
- No memory sharing, leading to underutilization of available memory.

Example: *Early operating systems like MS-DOS allocated memory in a single partition.*

2. Multiple-Partition Allocation

(a) Fixed Partitioning

- Divides memory into fixed-sized blocks before execution.
- It is simple but can lead to internal fragmentation (wasted space within allocated memory).
- It works best when process sizes are known in advance.

Example: *IBM OS/360 used fixed partitioning to allocate memory.*

(b) Dynamic Partitioning

- Partitions are created dynamically based on process requirements.
- It eliminates internal fragmentation but can cause external fragmentation (small unused memory spaces between allocated blocks).
- Requires compaction techniques to consolidate free memory.

Example: *UNIX-based systems use dynamic partitioning for better memory efficiency.*

3. Paging

- Memory is divided into fixed-sized pages (typically 4KB each).
- Eliminates external fragmentation, as processes can be stored in non-contiguous memory locations.
- Requires a page table to map virtual addresses to physical memory.

  Example: *Windows and Linux use paging to manage memory efficiently.*

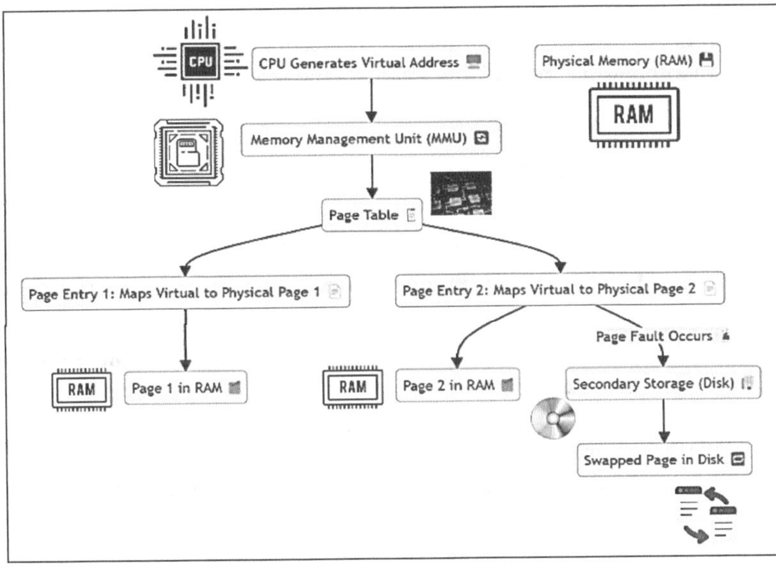

Figure 4.1: *Paging Mechanism and Page Table*

Figure 4.1 illustrates the Paging Mechanism and Page Table, a key component of virtual memory management used in modern operating systems.

Step-by-Step Process

1. CPU Generates a Virtual Address

- The CPU creates a virtual address, which needs to be translated into a physical memory address before accessing data.

2. Memory Management Unit (MMU) Processes the Request

- The virtual address is sent to the Memory Management Unit (MMU), which handles address translation.
- The MMU consults the Page Table, which contains mappings between **virtual pages and physical memory pages.**

3. Page Table Lookup

- If the required virtual page has a corresponding entry in physical memory (RAM), the system retrieves it:
  - **Page Entry 1** → Maps Virtual Page to Physical Page 1 (Page Hit).
  - **Page Entry 2** → Maps Virtual Page to Physical Page 2 (Page Hit).

4. Page Fault Handling

- If the requested page is not in RAM, a Page Fault occurs.
- The system retrieves the missing page from Secondary Storage (Disk), which holds swapped-out pages.

5. Swapping Pages from Disk to RAM

- The missing page is loaded into RAM, and the Page Table is updated accordingly.
- This process ensures efficient memory allocation, allowing multiple processes to run smoothly while minimizing fragmentation.

Advantages of Paging

- **Eliminates External Fragmentation** by allowing non-contiguous memory allocation.
- **Efficient Memory Usage** through dynamic page swapping.
- **Used in Modern OS (Windows/Linux)** for optimized performance and multitasking.

Paging is essential for managing memory efficiently in **multitasking environments**, ensuring smooth program execution while maximizing available physical memory.

4. Segmentation

- Divides memory into logical segments (e.g., code segment, data segment, stack segment).
- Segments are variable in size and correspond to logical program structures.
- It is more flexible than paging but may lead to external fragmentation.

  Example: *Used in Intel x86 architecture for memory management.*

Key Components of Segmentation

1. Process Segments

- A process (Process P) is divided into multiple segments (Segment 1, Segment 2, Segment 3, etc.), each representing a logical unit such as code, stack, or data.
- Segments are stored non-contiguously in main memory, reducing external fragmentation.

2. Segment Map Table

- Each process has a Segment Map Table that keeps track of:
  - Segment Number (SN) – Identifies different segments.
  - Size – Specifies the segment's memory requirement.
  - **Memory Address** – Indicates the starting location of the segment in the main memory.

3. Main Memory Allocation

- The **Operating System (OS)** maintains memory allocation.

- Each segment is stored at different physical addresses based on availability, as shown in the Main Memory column.
- For example, Segment 1 (Size: 400) is stored at memory location 100, and Segment 2 (Size: 200) is stored at memory location 500, allowing efficient space utilization.

Figure 4.2 illustrates Segmentation in Memory Management, a technique that divides a process into variable-sized segments instead of fixed-sized pages.

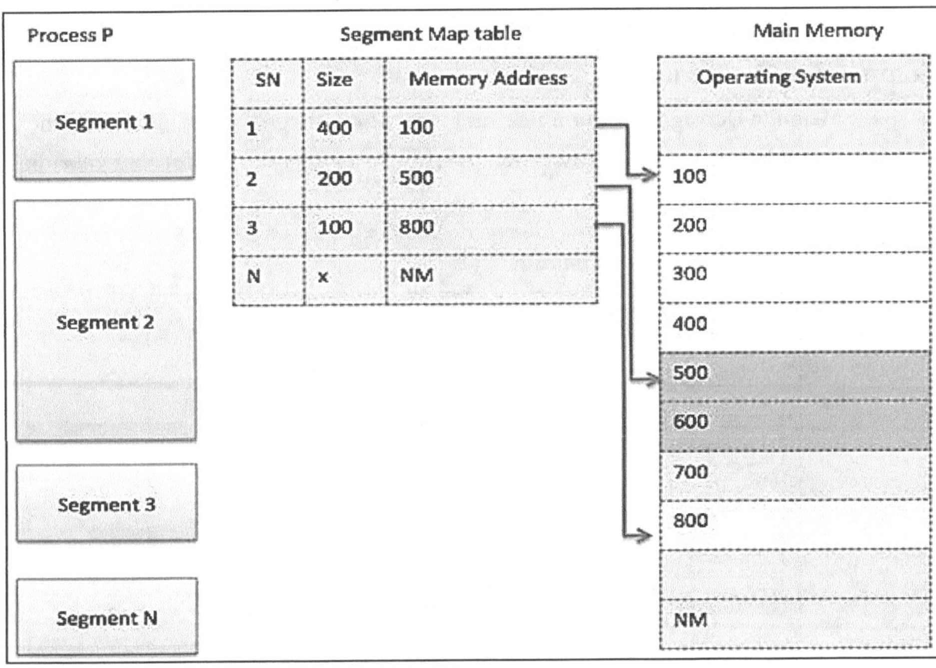

Figure 4.2: Segmentation in Memory Management

Advantages of Segmentation

- **Logical Program Structuring**: Code, data, and stack are stored as separate segments, improving memory organization.
- **Efficient Memory Utilization**: Reduces internal fragmentation since segments are variable-sized.
- **Flexible Allocation**: Each segment can grow dynamically, making it ideal for systems with variable-sized processes.

Disadvantages

- **External Fragmentation**: Over time, memory gets fragmented as segments of different sizes are loaded and removed.
- **Slower Access**: Since segments are stored non-contiguously, address translation requires additional memory lookups, impacting performance.

Segmentation is commonly used in multitasking operating systems and modern computing architectures to manage memory efficiently while maintaining logical separation between different program components.

Memory Fragmentation and Compaction

Memory fragmentation occurs when allocated memory blocks are separated by small unused spaces, reducing memory efficiency.

Types of Fragmentation

1. Internal Fragmentation: Memory wasted within allocated blocks.
2. External Fragmentation: Small gaps between allocated memory blocks.

Compaction Techniques

- **Memory Defragmentation:** Rearranging memory to group free blocks together.
- **Swapping:** Moving processes temporarily to disk (swap space) and reloading them.

  Example: *Windows Task Manager's Memory Optimization feature compacts fragmented memory dynamically.*

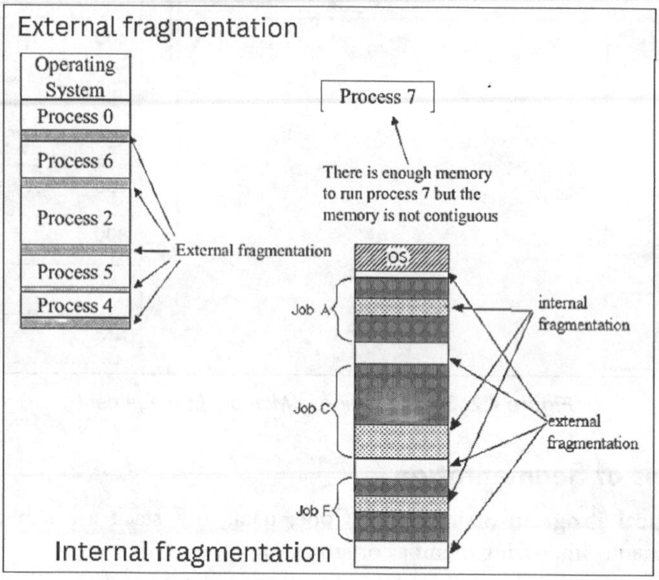

Figure 4.3: *Internal vs. External Fragmentation*

Figure 4.3 illustrates Internal vs. External Fragmentation, two types of memory inefficiencies that occur in memory allocation.

1. External Fragmentation

- It occurs when free memory blocks are scattered across the system due to non-contiguous allocation.
- Even if the total free memory is sufficient for a new process (Process 7 in the diagram), it cannot be allocated because the memory is fragmented.
- This is a major issue in dynamic memory allocation, leading to inefficient memory utilization.
- Solution: Compaction (rearranging memory blocks) or Paging (dividing memory into fixed-size pages).

2. Internal Fragmentation

- It occurs when allocated memory blocks have unused space because memory is assigned in fixed-sized units.
- For example, if a job requires 180 KB, but the system allocates a 200 KB block, the 20 KB difference is wasted.
- Solution: Using dynamic memory allocation instead of fixed block sizes.

Key Takeaways

- External fragmentation prevents large processes from being allocated even when enough memory is available.
- Internal fragmentation wastes memory inside allocated blocks due to fixed block sizes.
- Modern operating systems use paging and segmentation to minimize both types of fragmentation, improving memory efficiency.

Virtual Memory and Swapping

Virtual memory allows a system to use disk space as an extension of RAM, enabling the execution of programs larger than available physical memory.

Swapping Process

- Active processes are moved to disk (swap space) when memory is full.
- The system retrieves processes when needed, reducing memory pressure.
- Swapping improves multitasking but increases latency.

Example: *Linux uses a dedicated swap partition to manage virtual memory efficiently.*

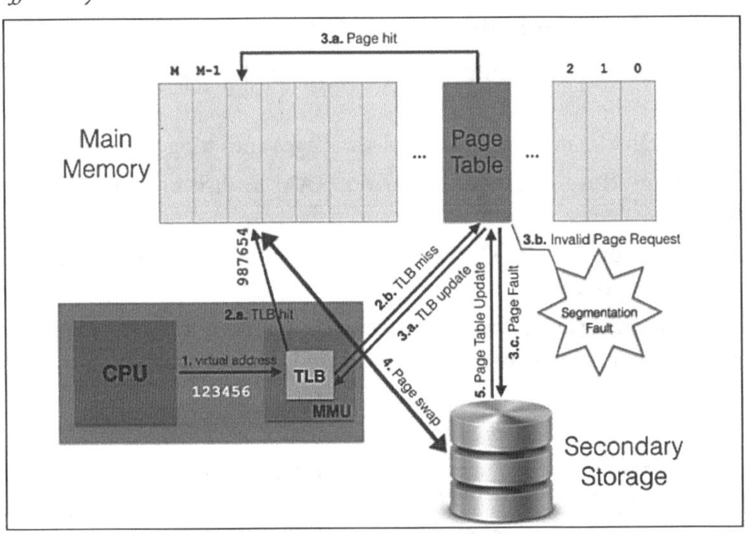

Figure 4.4: *Virtual Memory, Paging and Swapping Process*

Figure 4.4 illustrates the Virtual Memory, Paging, and Swapping Process, demonstrating how modern operating systems manage memory efficiently.

Step-by-Step Process

1. Virtual Address Translation

- The CPU generates a virtual address that must be translated into a physical address.
- This request first passes through the Translation Lookaside Buffer (TL(b) in the Memory Management Unit (MMU).

2. TLB Handling

- If the TLB contains the required page mapping (TLB hit), the translation occurs quickly (Step 2.(a).
- If the required page is not found in the TLB (TLB miss), the page table in the main memory is accessed (Step 2.(b), and the TLB is updated (Step 3.(a).

3. Page Table Lookup and Page Fault Handling

- If the requested page is in main memory (Page Hit, Step 3.(a), it is fetched immediately.
- If the requested page is not mapped in memory (Invalid Page Request, Step 3.(b), it causes a Segmentation Fault.
- If the page is valid but currently swapped out, a Page Fault (Step 3.(c) occurs, triggering a Page Table Update (Step 5).

4. Page Swapping from Secondary Storage

- When a Page Fault occurs, the missing page is retrieved from secondary storage (disk swap space) and loaded into main memory (Step 4).
- The updated page is then mapped in the Page Table, and execution resumes.

Key Concepts Demonstrated in the Diagram

- **Virtual Memory:** Extends available memory beyond physical RAM by using secondary storage.
- **Paging:** Divides memory into fixed-size pages and stores them efficiently in RAM.
- **Swapping:** Moves inactive pages from RAM to disk to free up space for active processes.
- **Segmentation Faults:** Occur when a program attempts to access an invalid memory region.

This memory management technique allows computers to run larger applications than available RAM, ensuring efficient multitasking and process isolation while minimizing memory wastage.

***Table 4.3:** Comparison of Memory Allocation Strategies*

Strategy	Pros	Cons
Fixed Partitioning	Simple to implement	Wastes memory due to internal fragmentation
Dynamic Partitioning	Efficient memory utilization	This leads to external fragmentation

Strategy	Pros	Cons
Paging	Eliminates external fragmentation	Requires a page table, increasing overhead
Segmentation	Logical memory management	Can suffer from external fragmentation

Table 4.3 compares different memory allocation strategies, highlighting their advantages and drawbacks. Fixed partitioning is simple but results in internal fragmentation, while dynamic partitioning efficiently utilizes memory but can cause external fragmentation. Paging eliminates external fragmentation by dividing memory into fixed-sized pages but requires a page table, increasing system overhead. Segmentation provides logical memory management, allowing programs to be divided into meaningful sections, but it can still suffer from external fragmentation.

Conclusion

Memory allocation strategies play a critical role in ensuring system stability, efficiency, and performance. Modern operating systems use a combination of paging, segmentation, and virtual memory to manage memory dynamically.

The following section will discuss Memory Caching Techniques, focusing on how caching enhances system speed and responsiveness.

4.3 MEMORY CACHING TECHNIQUES

Introduction to Memory Caching

Memory caching is a technique used to speed up data access and processing by storing frequently accessed data in a high-speed memory layer. A cache acts as an intermediary between the CPU, RAM, and storage devices, significantly reducing latency and improving system performance.

Caching is widely used in computer architecture, databases, web applications, and distributed systems to optimize efficiency and reduce load times. By implementing effective caching strategies, systems can minimize data retrieval delays and improve user experience.

Types of Cache Memory

Cache memory is classified into several types based on **location and function**:

1. Processor Cache (CPU Cache)

- It is located inside the CPU and provides high-speed access to frequently used instructions.
- Reduces the need to fetch data from RAM, enhancing execution speed.
- Includes multiple levels:
    - **L1 Cache (Level 1):** Smallest but fastest, located closest to the CPU cores.
    - **L2 Cache (Level 2):** Larger but slightly slower than L1.
    - **L3 Cache (Level 3):** Shared among CPU cores, improving overall performance.

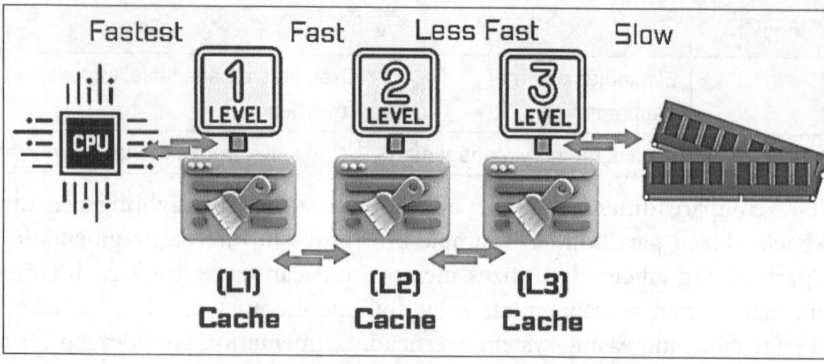

Figure 4.7: CPU Cache Levels (L1, L2, L3)

Figure 38 illustrates the CPU Cache Levels (L1, L2, L3), which play a crucial role in improving processor performance by reducing memory access latency.

Hierarchy of Cache Levels

1. L1 Cache (Level 1) – Fastest

- Located **inside** the CPU core.
- Smallest in size (typically 32KB – 256KB per core).
- Stores frequently accessed instructions and data for ultra-fast retrieval.
- **Speed:** Fastest, as it is directly connected to the CPU.

2. L2 Cache (Level 2) – Fast

- Larger than L1 but slower (256KB – 8MB per core).
- Located inside or near the CPU core.
- Acts as a secondary buffer, storing additional temporary data.
- **Speed:** Slower than L1 but still much faster than RAM.

3. L3 Cache (Level 3) – Less Fast

- Shared among multiple CPU cores.
- Much larger (4MB – 64M(b), optimizing multi-core performance.
- It helps prevent memory bottlenecks by improving data access speed.
- **Speed:** Slower than L1 and L2 but significantly faster than RAM.

4. RAM (Main Memory) – Slowest

- Located outside the CPU, accessed when data is not found in L1, L2, or L3.
- **Speed:** Much slower compared to cache memory.

Why Cache Matters?

- Reduces CPU waiting time by storing frequently accessed data.
- Improves processing speed and efficiency.
- Ensures smooth execution of programs by minimizing RAM dependency.

Key Takeaway

The cache memory hierarchy balances speed and size, ensuring that the CPU accesses the fastest memory possible while efficiently managing larger data sets across different cache levels.

2. Disk Cache (Storage Cache)

- Stores frequently accessed data from HDDs or SSDs.
- Reduces the number of disk read/write operations, increasing overall system efficiency.
- Uses RAM or a dedicated NAND flash cache for fast access.

Example: *SSDs with DRAM cache significantly enhance data retrieval speeds compared to non-cached SSDs.*

3. Web Cache (Browser & Proxy Cache)

- Stores copies of frequently accessed web pages, images, and scripts.
- Reduces bandwidth usage and speeds up web browsing.
- Implemented at multiple levels:
  - **Browser Cache:** Saves data locally on the user's device.
  - **Proxy Cache:** Caches web content at the network level for multiple users.

Example: *Google Chrome and Mozilla Firefox use local caching to improve webpage loading times.*

4. Database Cache

- Speeds up query execution by storing frequently accessed database records.
- Reduces CPU and disk I/O load.
- Utilizes techniques such as in-memory caching, query result caching, and index caching.

Example: MySQL, PostgreSQL, and Redis use caching mechanisms to optimize database queries.

Cache Mapping Techniques

Cache memory is organized using mapping techniques that determine how data is stored and retrieved:

1. Direct-Mapped Cache

- Each memory block maps to a specific cache location.
- It is simple but may cause frequent cache misses (conflicts).

2. Fully Associative Cache

- Any memory block can be placed anywhere in the cache.
- High flexibility but requires more complex hardware logic.

3. Set-Associative Cache

- Memory blocks are mapped into sets of cache lines.
- Provides a balance between direct-mapped and fully associative caching.

The following **Figure 4.8** illustrates the differences between Direct-Mapped, Set-Associative, and Fully Associative Cache Mapping techniques, which determine how memory blocks are mapped into the cache. In a Direct-Mapped Cache, each memory block is mapped to a single specific cache line based on its block number. The index in the cache is determined using modulo arithmetic (e.g., Block # 5 is mapped to Cache Line 5). While this method is simple and fast, it suffers from a high cache conflict rate if multiple blocks map to the same cache line.

In contrast, a Set-Associative Cache divides memory blocks into sets, with each set containing multiple cache lines. A block can be placed in any line within a specific set, reducing conflicts compared to a direct-mapped cache. The search process is more efficient, as it checks only within the assigned set. This technique provides a balanced trade-off between speed and conflict reduction but is more complex than direct-mapped caching.

On the other hand, a Fully Associative Cache allows a memory block to be placed anywhere in the cache, not restricted to a specific set or line. This approach minimizes cache misses but requires associative searching across all cache lines, making it computationally expensive and slower.

Overall, the Direct-Mapped Cache is simple but prone to conflicts, the Set-Associative Cache balances speed and efficiency, and the Fully Associative Cache provides flexibility at the cost of higher complexity. Modern processors commonly use set-associative caching to achieve an optimal balance between performance and cost, ensuring efficient memory access and improved CPU speed.

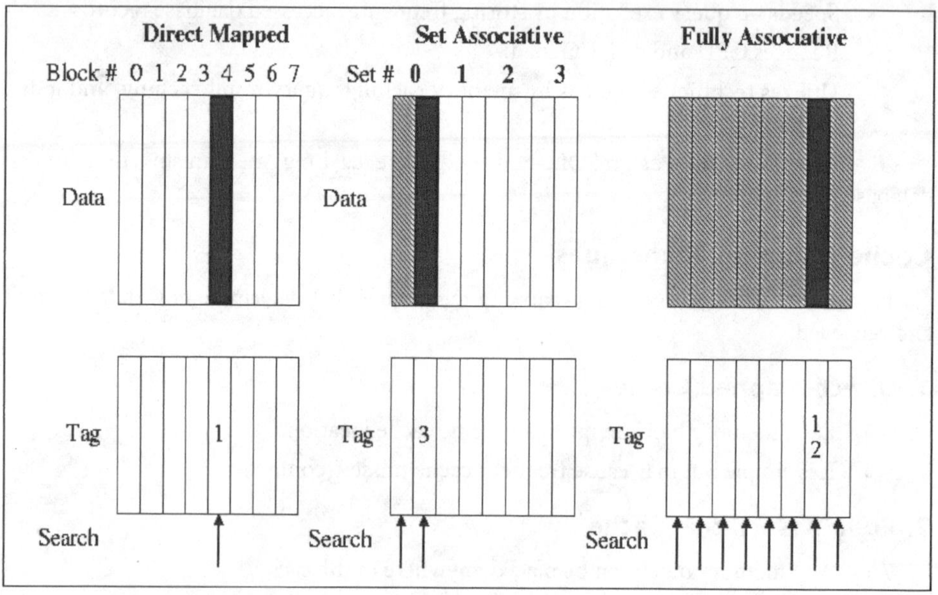

***Figure 4.8:** Direct-Mapped vs. Fully Associative vs. Set-Associative Cache*

Cache Replacement Policies

When a cache is full, the system must evict old data to make room for new data. Common cache replacement algorithms include:

1. Least Recently Used (LRU)

- Replaces the least recently accessed item.
- It is commonly used in CPU caching and virtual memory management.

2. First-In, First-Out (FIFO)

- Evicts the oldest data first, regardless of access frequency.
- Simple but may not always retain valuable data.

3. Least Frequently Used (LFU)

- Removes the least accessed items over time.
- It is more intelligent than FIFO but requires additional tracking overhead.

Example: *Modern web browsers use LRU to manage page caching efficiently.*

Cache Optimization Strategies

Effective cache optimization improves performance and resource utilization. Techniques include:

- **Prefetching:** Predicting and loading data before it is requested.
- **Write-Back vs. Write-Through Policies:** Balancing data consistency and speed.
- **Adaptive Caching:** Dynamically adjusting cache size based on workload.
- **Cache Partitioning:** Dividing cache into sections to prioritize critical data.

Example: *AI-driven caching algorithms in cloud computing dynamically adjust cache policies for optimal performance.*

Table 4.5: *Comparison of Cache Techniques*

Cache Type	Speed	Size	Application
L1 Cache	Fastest	Small	CPU instruction execution
L2 Cache	Fast	Medium	CPU multi-core processing
Disk Cache	Moderate	Large	Storage optimization
Web Cache	Variable	Depends on browser settings	Web page loading

Table 4.5 compares different cache techniques based on speed, size, and application. L1 Cache is the fastest and smallest, directly assisting in CPU instruction execution. L2 Cache, though slightly slower, is more extensive and helps with multi-core processing efficiency. Disk Cache improves storage performance by temporarily storing frequently accessed data from HDDs or SSDs. Web Cache, which varies in size, enhances web browsing speed by storing previously loaded web pages, reducing the need to re-download content.

Conclusion

Memory caching is an essential technique for enhancing computing efficiency, reducing latency, and improving system performance. By implementing efficient cache mapping, replacement policies, and optimization strategies, systems can handle workloads faster and more efficiently.

The following section will discuss Memory Management in Modern Operating Systems, focusing on how different OS platforms implement memory management and caching techniques.

4.4 MEMORY MANAGEMENT IN MODERN OPERATING SYSTEMS

Introduction to OS-Based Memory Management

Modern operating systems (OS) utilize sophisticated memory management techniques to allocate, track, and optimize system memory efficiently. Memory management in an OS ensures stable performance, multitasking, security, and process isolation.

Different OS platforms, such as Windows, Linux, and macOS, implement unique approaches to memory management, balancing performance and resource efficiency.

Core Functions of Memory Management in an OS

A modern OS handles memory management through several key functions:

1. Process Address Space Management

- Allocates virtual memory to each process, ensuring isolation.
- Uses paging and segmentation to manage address spaces efficiently.

2. Memory Allocation and Deallocation

- Dynamically assigns memory blocks to processes.
- Reclaims unused memory using garbage collection (in managed environments like Java and .NET).

3. Memory Protection

- Prevents unauthorized access between processes.
- Implements access control policies and privilege levels.

4. Swapping and Virtual Memory Management

- It uses disk-based swapping when physical memory (RAM) is full.
- Manages swap files (Windows) or swap partitions (Linux) to extend memory.

Memory Management in Windows OS

Windows operating systems use hybrid memory management techniques combining paging, segmentation, and dynamic allocation.

Key Features

- Implements a virtual memory manager (VMM) to manage RAM efficiently.

- It uses a page file (pagefile.sys) to swap inactive memory pages to disk.
- Supports dynamic memory allocation with demand paging.
- It uses memory compression to optimize RAM usage.

  Example: *Windows Task Manager displays real-time memory usage, including committed memory, cached memory, and available memory.*

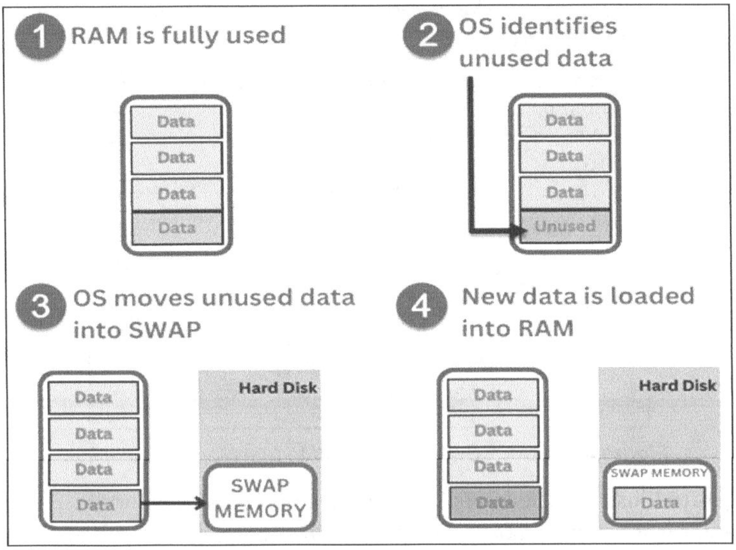

Figure 4.9: *Windows Memory Paging and Swap File Mechanism*

Figure 4.9 illustrates the Windows Memory Paging and Swap File Mechanism, a process used by the operating system to manage memory efficiently when RAM becomes full.

When RAM is fully utilized (Step 1), the operating system needs to free up space for new processes. It does this by identifying unused or less frequently accessed data (Step 2) within the memory. The OS then moves this inactive data into the swap file (Step 3), which is stored on the hard disk or SSD in a designated area called Swap Memory (Pagefile in Windows).

Once the swap operation is completed, new data can be loaded into RAM (Step 4), allowing active applications to run smoothly. The swap file serves as a temporary storage location for inactive memory pages, ensuring that the system does not run out of RAM.

This mechanism is essential for multitasking, as it enables systems to run more applications than the available physical memory can accommodate. However, swap memory is significantly slower than RAM, leading to performance degradation when excessive paging occurs. Optimizing RAM usage and minimizing swap dependency can enhance overall system performance.

Memory Management in Linux OS

Linux OS employs a flexible and efficient memory management system, making it ideal for servers and cloud computing.

Key Features

- It uses demand paging with lazy loading to allocate memory efficiently.

- Implements a swap partition or swap file to extend RAM capacity.
- Supports kernel-based memory allocation (kmalloc, slab allocators) for system performance tuning.
- Utilizes Transparent Huge Pages (THP) to reduce paging overhead and boost performance.
- Provides OOM (Out-of-Memory) Killer, which terminates low-priority processes when RAM is exhausted.

Example: *Linux systems can optimize memory allocation through /proc/meminfo and free command.*

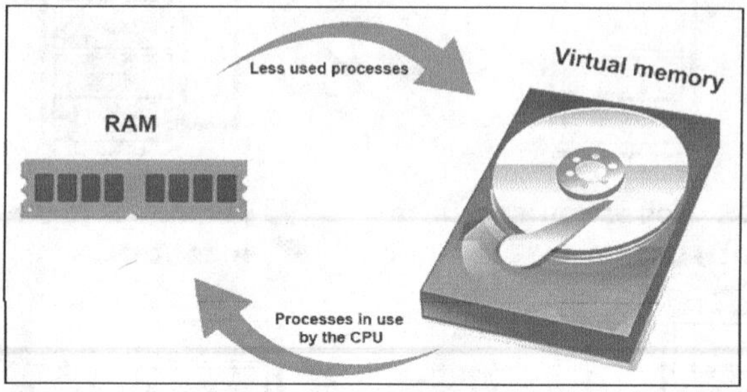

Figure 4.10: Linux Swap Space and Virtual Memory Mapping

Figure 4.10 illustrates the Linux Swap Space and Virtual Memory Mapping, a crucial mechanism for managing memory when physical RAM is fully utilized.

In this process, the operating system moves less frequently used processes from RAM to Virtual Memory (Swap Space) on the hard disk or SSD. This allows more critical processes to remain in RAM, where access speeds are significantly faster. When these swapped-out processes are needed again, they are brought back into RAM, replacing less frequently used data. Linux efficiently manages swap space using paging and swapping techniques, ensuring that system performance remains stable even under high memory loads. However, because disk-based swap memory is much slower than RAM, excessive swapping can slow down system performance.

To optimize swap usage, Linux allows users to configure swappiness (swap usage preference) and use faster SSD-based swap partitions. This technique is essential for multitasking, running large applications, and preventing system crashes due to out-of-memory conditions.

Memory Management in macOS

macOS employs a unified memory architecture (UM(a) for optimized resource sharing between CPU and GPU.

Key Features

- It uses demand paging with prefetching for efficiency.
- Implements memory compression to optimize RAM usage.
- Uses a Unified Buffer Cache (UB(c) to improve file system access.
- Supports automatic memory management and garbage collection in specific applications.

***Example:** The macOS Activity Monitor provides real-time tracking of memory usage, swap usage, and compressed memory.*

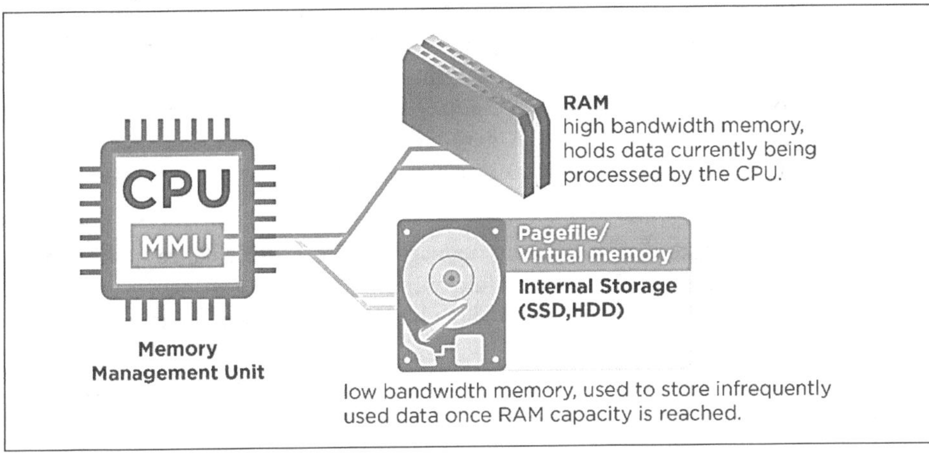

***Figure 4.11:** macOS Unified Memory Architecture*

Figure 4.11 illustrates the macOS Unified Memory Architecture (UM(a), which optimizes memory allocation between RAM and virtual memory.

In macOS, RAM (high-bandwidth memory) holds actively processed data, ensuring fast access speeds for CPU operations. When RAM capacity is fully utilized, the system moves infrequently used data to virtual memory (pagefile) stored on SSD or HDD, allowing the system to continue functioning smoothly without crashing due to memory exhaustion. This process is managed by the Memory Management Unit (MMU), which dynamically allocates resources between RAM and internal storage.

Unlike traditional memory management, macOS Unified Memory Architecture (UM(a) allows the CPU and GPU to share the same memory pool, improving efficiency and reducing latency. This seamless integration enhances multitasking, graphics rendering, and system performance, particularly in Apple's M1 and M2 chips. However, since SSD-based virtual memory is slower than RAM, frequent swapping can impact performance.

To optimize memory usage, macOS employs advanced memory compression, efficient swap algorithms, and fast SSD storage, ensuring a balance between performance and resource utilization in demanding tasks such as video editing, software development, and multitasking workflows.

***Table 4.6:** Comparison of Memory Management in Windows, Linux,* and macOS

Feature	Windows	Linux	macOS
Paging	Yes	Yes	Yes
Swap Space	Pagefile.sys	Swap Partition	Swap File
Memory Compression	Yes	Yes	Yes
Unified Memory Model	No	No	Yes
Demand Paging	Yes	Yes	Yes
OOM Handling	Limited	OOM Killer	Automatic

Table 4.6 compares memory management features across Windows, Linux, and macOS, highlighting their approaches to paging, swap space, memory compression, and out-of-memory (OOM) handling. All three operating systems support paging and memory compression, but their swap space implementations differ, with Windows using Pagefile.sys, Linux relies on a dedicated swap partition, and macOS utilizes a swap file. macOS features a unified memory model, allowing the CPU and GPU to share memory dynamically. At the same time, Linux implements an OOM Killer for better process management compared to Windows' limited OOM handling mechanisms.

Conclusion

Modern operating systems dynamically manage memory to balance performance, multitasking, and resource allocation. While Windows, Linux, and macOS implement unique approaches, they share core functionalities like paging, virtual memory management, and memory compression.

The following section will explore Memory Performance Optimization Techniques, detailing best practices to enhance memory efficiency and responsiveness.

Interesting Facts

- **Speed Boosters:** Caching is often referred to as "the accelerator" of computing systems because it dramatically reduces the time needed to access frequently used data.
- **Multi-Level Magic:** Modern CPUs employ multiple cache levels (L1, L2, L3), each optimized for different speeds and sizes, to ensure that the most critical data is available almost instantly.
- **Universal Strategy:** Beyond processors, caching is used in disks, web browsers, databases, and even distributed systems—making it a universal solution to speed up data retrieval across diverse applications.

Video Resources

- **Overview Videos:** Search for "Memory Caching Explained" or "How CPU Caches Work" on YouTube for animated guides that illustrate cache hierarchies (L1, L2, L3) and their roles.
- **Tutorials:** Look for detailed walkthroughs such as "Understanding Disk Cache and Web Cache" and "Cache Replacement Policies (LRU, FIFO, LFU)" to see practical examples.
- **Expert Panels:** Channels like *Computerphile* and *Techquickie* often discuss the impact of caching on system performance and provide insights into emerging caching algorithms.

Use of ICT

- **Real-Time Optimization:** ICT tools, such as performance monitors and diagnostic software (e.g., Windows Resource Monitor, Linux's vmstat), help track cache hit rates and identify bottlenecks.
- **Adaptive Algorithms:** Modern ICT systems use AI-powered caching algorithms that dynamically adjust cache sizes and policies based on current workload patterns.

- **Distributed Caching:** In cloud and distributed environments, caching systems (like Redis or Memcache(d) are essential for reducing database load and speeding up web applications, ensuring a smooth user experience.

Applications (Real Life/Industrial)

- **Personal Computing:** Local CPU and disk caches enable faster boot times and smoother operation for everyday tasks such as web browsing, gaming, and multimedia editing.
- **Enterprise and Data Centers:** Large-scale web applications and database systems use caching to minimize latency and handle millions of transactions per second.
- **Web Browsing:** Browser caches store frequently visited pages, images, and scripts, reducing load times and saving bandwidth.
- **Industrial Systems:** Embedded systems in automotive controls and manufacturing equipment utilize caching to ensure real-time performance and system reliability.

Case Study (Environmental/Sustainability/Social/Ethical Issues)

Context

A multinational e-commerce company was facing high energy consumption and increased hardware wear in its data centres due to frequent disk accesses and inefficient database queries.

Scenario

- **Challenge:** The company's servers were overloading during peak times, leading to excessive use of disk I/O and increased cooling requirements, thereby raising energy costs and the overall environmental footprint.
- **Solution:**
  - **Implementation of In-Memory Caching:** The company deployed a distributed caching system (using Redis) to store frequently accessed product information and user sessions.
  - **AI-Driven Cache Optimization:** By integrating adaptive caching algorithms, the system dynamically adjusted cache size and replacement policies, significantly reducing disk I/O.
  - **Energy Efficiency:** This reduced the load on physical storage systems and decreased cooling demands, contributing to lower energy consumption and operational costs.
- **Impact:**
  - **Performance Boost:** The caching solution improved page load times and reduced latency during high-traffic periods.
  - **Environmental Benefit:** The reduction in disk usage and cooling needs led to a measurable decrease in energy consumption, aligning with the company's sustainability goals.
  - **Ethical Consideration:** By optimizing resource use, the company demonstrated social responsibility in minimizing its carbon footprint and promoting sustainable business practices.

Discussion Points

- In what ways can caching contribute to energy efficiency and sustainability in large data centres?
- How does efficient caching reduce the strain on hardware, thereby extending its lifespan and reducing electronic waste?
- What are the ethical implications for companies that invest in performance-enhancing yet environmentally friendly technologies?

Create Inquisitiveness and Curiosity

- **Speculative Inquiry:** How might emerging technologies like AI-driven predictive caching reshape the future of data centres and cloud computing?
- **Design Challenge:** Imagine designing a caching system for a space mission where communication latency is extreme. What strategies would you use to ensure data availability and speed?
- **Debate Prompt:** Should systems favour a larger cache with less frequent replacements (e.g., LFU) over a simpler approach (e.g., FIFO) if energy conservation is a primary goal? What are the trade-offs?
- **Innovation Brainstorm:** Can we conceptualize a hybrid caching model that integrates local and distributed caching to optimize both speed and environmental sustainability?

Solved Problems (With Increasing Difficulty Level)

Problem 1 (Basic)

Question

What is the primary purpose of a CPU cache?

Solution

The primary purpose of a CPU cache is to store frequently accessed instructions and data close to the processor, thereby reducing the time needed to access memory and increasing processing speed.

Problem 2 (Intermediate)

Question

Explain the difference between direct-mapped and set-associative cache mapping techniques.

Solution

- **Direct-Mapped Cache:** Each memory block is mapped to precisely one cache line, which is simple but can lead to frequent cache misses due to conflicts.
- **Set-Associative Cache:** Memory blocks are grouped into sets, and each block can be placed in any line within its designated set. This method offers a balance between complexity and cache hit rate, reducing the likelihood of conflicts compared to direct-mapped caches.

Problem 3 (Advanced)

Question

Discuss the impact of cache replacement policies (such as LRU and LFU) on system performance. Provide an example scenario where one policy might be preferred over the other.

Solution

- **LRU (Least Recently Use(d):** Replaces the cache entry that has not been used for the longest time. It is effective when recent access patterns predict future use, making it suitable for general-purpose applications.
- **LFU (Least Frequently Use(d):** Evicts the entry that has been used the least number of times over a period. This policy is beneficial when certain data is accessed repeatedly over a long duration.

Example

In a web server environment, LRU might be preferred if user access patterns are highly variable, ensuring that the most recent and likely-to-be-requested pages remain cached. Conversely, LFU could be advantageous in a database cache where certain records are consistently accessed over time, preserving high-frequency data.

Problem 4 (Challenging)

Question

A distributed cloud service is experiencing increased latency during peak usage times. Propose a caching strategy that leverages both local (edge) caching and centralized caching to optimize performance and reduce energy consumption. Explain your approach and potential challenges.

Solution

A viable strategy would be to implement a hybrid caching system:

- **Edge Caching:** Deploy local caches (using systems like Redis or Memcache(d) at data centre edge locations to store frequently accessed content close to the end users. This reduces the distance data must travel, lowering latency and network load.
- **Centralized Caching:** Use a centralized cache layer to manage less frequently accessed but still critical data. This layer can benefit from AI-driven cache optimization to dynamically adjust the cache based on real-time demand and usage patterns.

Advantages

- **Reduced Latency:** Edge caching minimizes round-trip time, enhancing user experience during peak loads.
- **Energy Efficiency:** By decreasing the load on centralized servers and reducing data transmission distances, energy consumption is lowered.

Challenges

- **Cache Consistency:** Maintaining synchronization between edge and centralized caches can be complex, especially under high update frequencies.
- **Scalability:** As the user base grows, ensuring that edge caches have sufficient capacity without becoming a bottleneck can require careful resource planning.

Justification

This hybrid approach balances fast local access with the robustness of centralized management, effectively reducing overall latency and energy use while providing scalable performance during peak usage.

4.5 MEMORY PERFORMANCE OPTIMIZATION TECHNIQUES

Introduction to Memory Optimization

Memory performance optimization is crucial for ensuring efficient system performance, reduced latency, and enhanced multitasking capabilities. Proper optimization prevents memory leaks, fragmentation, and excessive paging, leading to smoother user experiences and better resource utilization.

Modern operating systems and applications implement several optimization techniques to enhance memory management efficiency, ranging from manual tuning to AI-driven automation.

Key Memory Optimization Techniques

1. Efficient Memory Allocation Strategies

- Use dynamic memory allocation (malloc, calloc, realloc in C/C++) to optimize resource usage.
- Prefer stack allocation over heap allocation for better performance.
- Use slab allocators in kernel-based applications to reduce fragmentation.

  Example: Linux uses kmalloc and slab allocation to optimize kernel memory allocation.

2. Memory Compression

- Reduces RAM consumption by compressing inactive memory pages.
- Speeds up multitasking by keeping more data in RAM instead of swapping to disk.
- Implemented in Windows (Memory Compression), macOS (Compressed Memory), and Linux (Zswap, ZRAM).

  Example: macOS uses compressed memory pages to reduce swap file usage and improve responsiveness.

In this process, the Main RAM holds data that is actively used, while ZRAM (compressed RAM) is utilized as an intermediate memory storage area. When memory usage increases, the operating system compresses inactive data and moves it into ZRAM, reducing the need for disk-based swapping. This helps in minimizing performance slowdowns caused by frequent disk swaps.

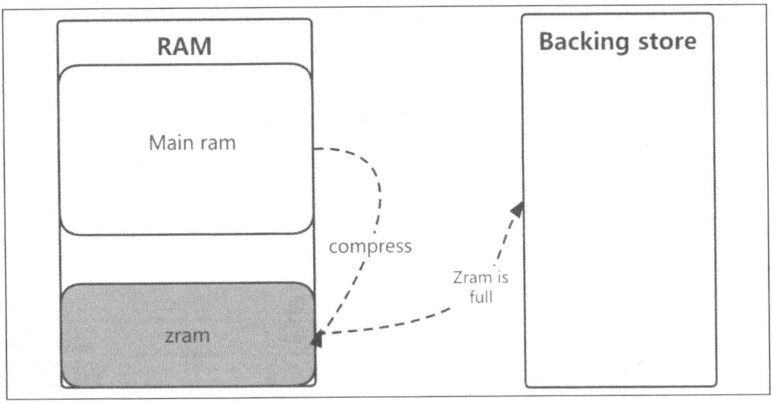

Figure 4.12: Memory Compression Mechanism in an OS

Figure 4.12 illustrates the Memory Compression Mechanism in an OS, a technique used to optimize RAM usage by storing compressed data in memory before swapping it to disk.

However, if ZRAM becomes full, the system transfers compressed pages to the Backing Store (disk-based swap space), ensuring that memory-intensive applications continue running without interruption. Since reading from and writing to ZRAM is significantly faster than accessing disk swap space, this approach enhances system performance, particularly in low-RAM environments, mobile devices, and Linux-based systems.

Modern operating systems, including Linux (ZRAM), Windows (Memory Compression), and macOS (Compressed Memory), implement similar mechanisms to optimize RAM efficiency, reduce paging, and improve multitasking performance.

3. Virtual Memory Optimization

- Adjusts swap file size dynamically based on system load.
- Reduces page faults by prefetching frequently used data.
- Uses fast SSDs for swap space to minimize performance degradation.

  Example: Windows and Linux allow users to configure custom swap space sizes for optimized performance.

4. Caching Mechanisms for Faster Data Access

- It uses disk caching to store frequently accessed data in RAM.
- Implements CPU cache optimizations (L1, L2, L3 caching) to speed up instruction execution.
- Uses AI-driven predictive caching in cloud environments for load balancing.

  For example, AI-powered caching in AWS and Google Cloud improves storage and memory performance.

Figure 4.13 illustrates the CPU and Disk Caching Mechanisms, which improve system performance by reducing redundant data retrieval operations.

In CPU caching, frequently accessed instructions and data are stored in L1, L2, and L3 cache memory, allowing the processor to retrieve them quickly instead of accessing slower RAM. This significantly reduces latency and enhances processing speed. Similarly, disk caching involves storing frequently accessed files in a faster memory location, such as SSD cache or RAM cache, reducing the need for repeated disk reads.

The diagram shows how a client (CPU or system request) first accesses data from an origin server (RAM or disk storage). During the first request, the caching server (CPU cache or disk cache) fetches the asset and stores it locally. In subsequent requests, instead of retrieving the data from the origin server, the cached data is delivered directly, leading to faster response times.

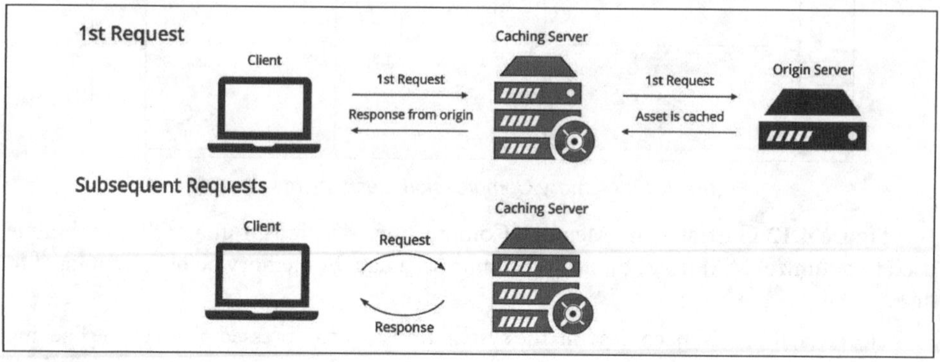

Figure 4.13: CPU and Disk Caching Mechanisms

By utilizing CPU and disk caching, systems can significantly enhance performance, lower response times, and reduce workload on primary storage components, making it essential for high-performance computing, databases, and web content delivery networks (CDNs).

5. Minimizing Memory Fragmentation

- It uses heap compaction and defragmentation techniques to consolidate free memory blocks.
- Prefers contiguous memory allocation when possible to reduce fragmentation.
- Allocates large memory blocks upfront to minimize dynamic memory resizing overhead.

  Example: Windows employs background memory defragmentation to optimize RAM usage.

6. Memory Leak Prevention and Garbage Collection

- Uses automated garbage collection (G(c) in Java, Python, and C# to reclaim unused memory.
- Employs manual deallocation (free, delete) in C and C++ to prevent memory leaks.
- Monitors heap usage to detect and resolve leaks in long-running applications.

  Example: JVM and .NET CLR use garbage collection algorithms to clean up unused objects periodically.

Table 4.7 outlines best practices for memory optimization, highlighting techniques that enhance system performance and efficiency. Memory compression helps reduce RAM consumption, while virtual memory tuning optimizes disk swapping to prevent slowdowns. Caching accelerates data retrieval, improving system responsiveness. Fragmentation reduction ensures efficient memory allocation, minimizing wasted space. Garbage collection prevents memory leaks and crashes, ensuring stable application performance.

***Table 4.7:** Best Practices for Memory Optimization*

Optimization Technique	Benefit
Memory Compression	Reduces RAM consumption
Virtual Memory Tuning	Minimizes disk swapping overhead
Caching	Speeds up data retrieval
Fragmentation Reduction	Improves memory allocation efficiency
Garbage Collection	Prevents memory leaks and crashes

Conclusion

Memory performance optimization enhances system stability, responsiveness, and resource utilization. By implementing memory compression, efficient allocation, caching, and fragmentation control, modern operating systems and applications can run faster and more efficiently.

The following section will provide a Unit Summary, Exercises, and Teacher's Know More, reinforcing the key concepts covered in Memory Management and Optimization.

Interesting Facts

- **Speed Booster:** Memory optimization techniques can significantly reduce latency by keeping more data available in fast RAM instead of slower disk-based storage.
- **Compression in Action:** Modern operating systems compress inactive memory pages to allow more applications to run simultaneously without resorting to disk swapping.
- **Fragmentation Fighters:** Techniques like heap compaction and slab allocation help in reducing memory fragmentation, ensuring that processes have access to contiguous memory blocks for improved performance.

Video Resources

- **Overview Videos:** Search for "Memory Performance Optimization Techniques" or "How Memory Compression Works" on YouTube for animated guides that explain these methods.
- **Tutorials:** Look for "Optimizing Virtual Memory in Windows/Linux" or "Understanding Cache and Fragmentation" to see practical examples of tuning and defragmentation.
- **Expert Discussions:** Channels such as *Computerphile* and *Techquickie* frequently cover topics like garbage collection, caching mechanisms, and dynamic memory allocation strategies.

Use of ICT

- **Monitoring Tools:** ICT systems use performance monitors (like Windows Resource Monitor Linux's top/htop) to track memory usage, detect leaks, and assess fragmentation levels.

- **Automated Optimization:** Modern operating systems leverage AI-driven predictive caching and memory compression techniques to adjust resource allocation in real-time.
- **Development Environments:** Programming IDEs now integrates memory profilers and garbage collection analysis tools, helping developers optimize their applications and reduce memory overhead.

Applications (Real Life / Industrial)

- **Personal Computing:** Memory optimization ensures faster application loading times and smoother multitasking on laptops and desktops.
- **Enterprise Servers:** Data centres rely on techniques like virtual memory tuning and caching to handle high volumes of transactions, reduce disk swapping, and lower energy consumption.
- **Embedded Systems:** In devices like automotive control units and IoT gadgets, efficient memory usage is critical for real-time operations and long-term reliability.
- **High-Performance Workstations:** Applications in video editing, scientific computing, and financial modelling benefit from reduced latency and efficient memory allocation, resulting in quicker data processing.

Case Study (Environmental/Sustainability/Social/Ethical Issues)

Context

A multinational financial services firm faced performance bottlenecks and increased energy consumption in its trading servers due to inefficient memory management and frequent disk swapping.

Scenario

- **Challenge:** The servers experienced high latency and overheating issues, leading to increased cooling demands and a larger carbon footprint.
- **Solution**
  - **Memory Compression:** The firm enabled OS-level memory compression (as implemented in Windows and Linux) to reduce reliance on disk swap, keeping more data in fast RAM.
  - **Virtual Memory Optimization:** They dynamically adjusted swap file sizes based on workload and upgraded to high-speed SSDs for swap space, significantly reducing page faults.
  - **Caching Enhancements:** AI-driven caching algorithms were deployed to prefetch frequently accessed data and reduce redundant disk operations.
- **Impact**
  - **Performance:** The optimizations resulted in smoother, faster trading operations with reduced latency.
  - **Sustainability:** Energy usage dropped due to lower disk activity and improved cooling efficiency, contributing to the firm's green IT initiatives.
  - **Ethical Aspect:** The firm set an industry benchmark for balancing high-performance computing with sustainable and socially responsible practices.

Discussion Points

- How can memory optimization contribute to reducing the overall energy footprint in data centres?
- What ethical considerations should companies have when optimizing systems to balance performance with environmental impact?
- In what ways can improved memory performance indirectly benefit end-users by lowering operational costs and carbon emissions?

Create Inquisitiveness and Curiosity

- **Future Possibilities:** How might emerging technologies like non-volatile RAM (NVRAM) or advanced AI-driven memory managers further revolutionize memory optimization?
- **Design Challenge:** Imagine we are designing a supercomputer for climate research. What memory optimization strategies would we incorporate to ensure both high performance and minimal energy consumption?
- **Debate:** Should system designers prioritize memory optimization for performance or energy efficiency? What are the trade-offs, and can a balanced approach be achieved?
- **Brainstorm:** Can we envision a new memory optimization technique that integrates dynamic cache partitioning with real-time compression adjustments based on workload predictions?

Solved Problems (With Increasing Difficulty Level)

Problem 1 (Basic)

Question

What is the primary benefit of using memory compression in modern operating systems?

Solution

Memory compression reduces RAM consumption by compressing inactive memory pages,which decreases the need for disk swapping and improves multitasking performance.

Problem 2 (Intermediate)

Question

How does virtual memory optimization improve system performance, and what role do high-speed SSDs play in this process?

Solution

Virtual memory optimization adjusts the swap file size dynamically based on system load and prefetches frequently used data, thereby reducing page faults. High-speed SSDs used for swap space minimize latency compared to traditional HDDs, leading to faster data retrieval and improved overall system responsiveness.

Problem 3 (Advanced)

Question

Compare the benefits and drawbacks of caching mechanisms versus memory defragmentation in the context of system performance optimization.

Solution

- **Caching Mechanisms**
  - *Benefits:* Accelerate data access by storing frequently accessed data in faster memory (e.g., CPU cache, disk cache), reducing latency.
  - *Drawbacks:* Additional management overhead is required, and it may become ineffective if cache coherence is not maintained.
- **Memory Defragmentation**
  - *Benefits:* Consolidates free memory blocks, reducing fragmentation and allowing larger contiguous memory allocations, which can enhance application performance.
  - *Drawbacks:* Defragmentation processes can be resource-intensive and may temporarily impact system performance during execution.

Problem 4 (Challenging)

Question

A high-performance computing centre is experiencing system slowdowns due to memory fragmentation and excessive swapping. Propose a comprehensive memory performance optimization strategy that includes efficient allocation, compression, and caching techniques. Justify your approach and discuss potential challenges.

Solution

A comprehensive strategy may include:

- **Efficient Memory Allocation**
  - Implement dynamic memory allocation strategies (using methods like slab allocation in kernel memory) to reduce fragmentation.
- **Memory Compression:**
  - Enable OS-level memory compression (such as Windows Memory Compression or Linux's ZRAM) to keep more data in RAM and reduce reliance on disk swapping.
- **Virtual Memory Tuning:**
  - Adjust swap file sizes dynamically and use high-speed SSDs for swap space to minimize the performance penalty of paging.
- **Caching Mechanisms**
  - Deploy AI-driven caching algorithms to prefetch frequently accessed data and optimize CPU cache utilization.
- **Fragmentation Reduction**
  - Schedule regular background defragmentation (or compaction) processes to consolidate free memory blocks and prevent performance degradation.

Justification

- This multi-layered approach addresses the core issues of memory fragmentation, inefficient allocation, and slow disk swapping.
- It leverages both hardware (high-speed SSDs) and software (compression, caching, dynamic allocation) improvements to deliver significant performance gains.

Challenges

- Integration of multiple techniques may increase system complexity.
- Continuous monitoring and fine-tuning are required to balance resource usage and avoid potential conflicts between optimization methods.

SUMMARY

This unit covered various memory management techniques, allocation strategies, caching mechanisms, and performance optimizations to ensure efficient resource utilization and improved system performance. The key topics discussed include:

- **Memory Management in Modern Operating Systems:** Differences in memory management strategies used by Windows, Linux, and macOS.
- **Memory Allocation Strategies:** Techniques such as paging, segmentation, and virtual memory.
- **Memory Caching:** Role of CPU cache, disk cache, web cache, and database caching in improving performance.
- **Memory Performance Optimization Techniques:** Methods to enhance memory efficiency, including compression, garbage collection, caching, and defragmentation.
- **Memory Leak Prevention:** Strategies such as automated garbage collection and heap monitoring.

EXERCISES

1. Subjective Questions (Conceptual and Analytical)

1. Compare and contrast paging and segmentation in memory management.
2. Explain how virtual memory enhances system performance.
3. Discuss the advantages and disadvantages of memory compression in modern operating systems.
4. How do caching mechanisms improve CPU and storage efficiency?
5. Describe the role of garbage collection in programming languages like Java and Python.
6. What are the key differences in memory allocation strategies between Windows and Linux?
7. How does memory fragmentation impact system performance, and how can it be minimized?
8. Explain how the OOM (Out-of-Memory) Killer works in Linux.
9. What is Transparent Huge Pages (THP), and how does it improve memory efficiency?
10. Describe how AI-driven memory optimization is transforming cloud computing.

2. Objective Questions (Multiple-Choice and True/False)

Multiple-choice questions (MCQs)

1. What is the primary function of virtual memory?
   (a) Increase CPU speed
   (b) Extend physical RAM using disk storage
   (c) Store temporary files
   (d) Increase battery life
2. Which of the following caching types is primarily used for **web browsing**?
   (a) CPU Cache
   (b) Web Cache
   (c) Disk Cache
   (d) RAM Cache
3. Memory fragmentation occurs when:
   (a) The system runs out of memory
   (b) Memory is allocated but not contiguous
   (c) Virtual memory is enabled
   (d) Page swapping is disabled
4. The OOM Killer in Linux is used to:
   (a) Allocate additional RAM
   (b) Reduce CPU usage
   (c) Terminate processes when memory runs low
   (d) Increase storage speed
5. Which memory allocation strategy eliminates external fragmentation?
   (a) Segmentation
   (b) Paging
   (c) Fixed Partitioning
   (d) Swapping

True/False Questions

1. Paging reduces external fragmentation by dividing memory into fixed-size blocks. *(True/False)*
2. Virtual memory increases physical RAM capacity. *(True/False)*
3. Memory compression is only available in Windows operating systems. *(True/False)*
4. Disk caching improves file access speed by keeping frequently used data in RAM. *(True/False)*
5. Transparent Huge Pages (THP) reduce memory overhead by increasing page sizes. *(True/False)*

TEACHER'S KNOW MORE

For educators and advanced learners, additional resources and insights include:

- **Advanced Paging Techniques:** Exploring demand paging, prefetching, and multi-level paging.
- **In-Depth Memory Management Comparisons:** How Windows, Linux, and macOS handle memory swapping, allocation, and kernel memory.
- **AI-Driven Memory Optimization:** Implementation of machine learning algorithms for predictive memory allocation.
- **Hands-on Labs:** Practical exercises on configuring swap space, memory compression, and heap debugging.
- **Future Trends in Memory Management:** Research on neuromorphic computing and persistent memory (PMEM).

This page is intentionally left blank!

5

ADVANCED STORAGE TECHNOLOGIES

UNIT

RATIONALE

In today's interconnected world, understanding network components is fundamental to designing, managing, and troubleshooting modern communication systems. This unit explores the basics of networking, the roles of various network infrastructures, and the critical differences between wired and wireless technologies. Students will gain hands-on knowledge of network cabling, communication media, and essential networking devices—such as hubs, switches, routers, and wireless access points—while also examining best practices in cable management and troubleshooting. The unit emphasizes both the theoretical concepts and practical applications of networking components, enabling learners to build robust network infrastructures that support efficient, secure, and scalable communications. It also prepares students to address real-world challenges in network security, device management, and wireless communication. It provides a solid foundation for advanced studies or professional roles in IT and networking.

OUTCOMES

By the end of this unit, students will be able to:

- **Understand Networking Fundamentals**
    - Describe the basics of networking and the various components that form a network infrastructure.
    - Differentiate between wired and wireless networking technologies.
- **Identify and Apply Networking Components**
    - Explain the roles and functions of key network devices, including hubs, switches, routers, modems, and wireless access points.
    - Distinguish between managed and unmanaged switches and their appropriate applications.
- **Analyze and Implement Network Cabling:**
    - Identify different types of Ethernet and fibre optic cables, including their categories, benefits, and applications.
    - Apply cable management best practices and perform basic tasks such as crimping and troubleshooting network cables.
- **Evaluate Wireless Communication and Security:**
    - Describe various Wi-Fi standards and configurations.
    - Understand and implement secure wireless communication methods, including the basics of point-to-point wireless networks.
    - Recognize the role of USB wireless devices and print servers in enhancing network connectivity.
- **Apply Practical Networking Solutions**
    - Integrate theoretical knowledge with hands-on activities to design, set up, and troubleshoot network infrastructures in diverse environments.

5.1 INTRODUCTION TO ADVANCED STORAGE TECHNOLOGIES

Overview of Modern Storage Solutions

As data generation continues to expand exponentially, traditional storage solutions like Hard Disk Drives (HDDs) and Solid-State Drives (SSDs) are evolving to keep up with increasing demands. Advanced storage technologies focus on higher performance, greater reliability, improved scalability, and enhanced data security.

These technologies include NVMe-based storage, cloud-based architectures, object storage, storage-class memory (SCM), and AI-driven storage optimization. Understanding these emerging technologies is crucial for organizations that require high-speed data processing, scalable infrastructure, and efficient data management.

Key Trends in Storage Technology

Modern storage solutions aim to address latency issues, storage density, durability, and data integrity. The following are some of the latest trends in storage technology:

1. NVMe (Non-Volatile Memory Express) and PCIe 5.0 Storage

- NVMe storage uses PCIe lanes for ultra-fast data access, reducing latency.
- PCIe 5.0-based storage solutions offer double the bandwidth compared to PCIe 4.0.
- NVMe SSDs outperform SATA-based SSDs in terms of speed and efficiency.

Example: High-performance computing (HP(c) environments and gaming systems utilize NVMe Gen4 and Gen5 SSDs.

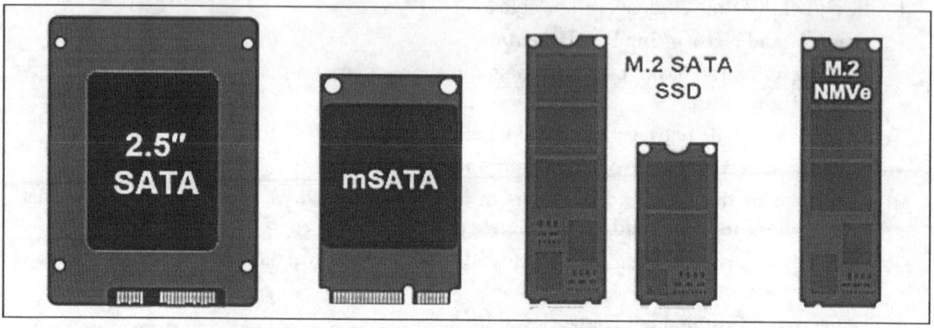

***Figure 5.1:** NVMe vs. SATA Performance Comparison*

Figure 5.1 illustrates the NVMe vs SATA Performance Comparison, highlighting the key differences in storage technologies used in modern computing.

SATA SSDs, including 2.5-inch SATA, mSATA, and M.2 SATA SSDs, use the Serial ATA (SAT(a) interface, which was initially designed for hard drives. These SSDs provide a significant speed boost over traditional HDDs, but they are limited by the SATA interface's bandwidth, which peaks at around 550 MB/s.

On the other hand, NVMe (Non-Volatile Memory Express) SSDs, such as M.2 NVMe, leverage the PCIe (Peripheral Component Interconnect Express) interface, enabling them to deliver speeds of up to 7000 MB/s in high-end models. NVMe drives operate with lower latency and higher throughput, making them ideal for gaming, video editing, high-performance computing, and enterprise workloads.

While SATA SSDs are still a cost-effective and reliable option for general users, NVMe SSDs provide superior performance, faster boot times, and reduced data transfer delays, making them the preferred choice for modern laptops, desktops, and servers.

2. Storage-Class Memory (SCM)

- A hybrid technology combining RAM speed with non-volatile storage.
- Used for persistent memory, allowing fast access to frequently used data.
- Reduces reliance on traditional DRAM and NAND storage, optimizing database processing and virtualization.

  Example: Intel Optane Persistent Memory accelerates database applications like MySQL and SAP HANA.

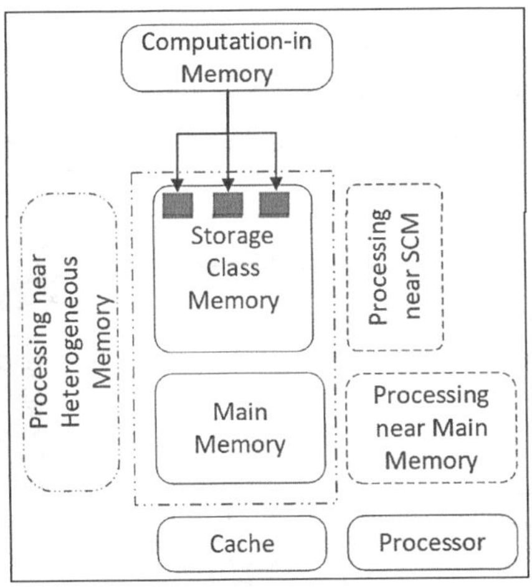

Figure 5.2: *Processing Option in Memory Hierarchy*

Figure 5.2 illustrates Processing Options in the Memory Hierarchy, showcasing different approaches to optimizing computation and memory access efficiency.

Computation-in-memory (CIM) is a technique that integrates processing capabilities directly within the Storage Class Memory (SCM) to reduce data movement bottlenecks. By executing computations closer to where the data resides, latency and power consumption are significantly minimized. This approach is beneficial for AI workloads, big data processing, and real-time analytics.

Another approach is Processing Near Memory (PNM), where computations are performed close to either Storage Class Memory (SCM) or Main Memory. This helps optimize data-intensive workloads by reducing the need for frequent interactions between the processor and traditional cache memory layers.

Additionally, Processing Near Heterogeneous Memory allows workload distribution across different types of memory technologies, ensuring better performance scaling and efficiency.

Overall, these memory-centric computing models enhance data processing speed, minimize power consumption, and improve efficiency in modern computing architectures, particularly in edge computing, AI accelerators, and high-performance computing (HP(c) environments.

3. AI-Driven Storage Optimization

- AI-enhanced storage systems use machine learning algorithms to predict data usage patterns.
- AI optimizes data placement, cache management, and storage tiering.
- Cloud providers like AWS and Google Cloud implement AI for smart storage allocation.

  Example: AI-driven caching improves cloud storage performance in content delivery networks (CDNs).

4. Object Storage for Big Data Applications

- Unlike traditional file systems, object storage organizes data in a flat structure.
- Provides scalability for cloud environments, IoT, and big data analytics.
- Ensures better data redundancy, security, and accessibility across multiple devices.

  For example, Amazon S3 and Google Cloud Storage use object storage to handle massive unstructured datasets.

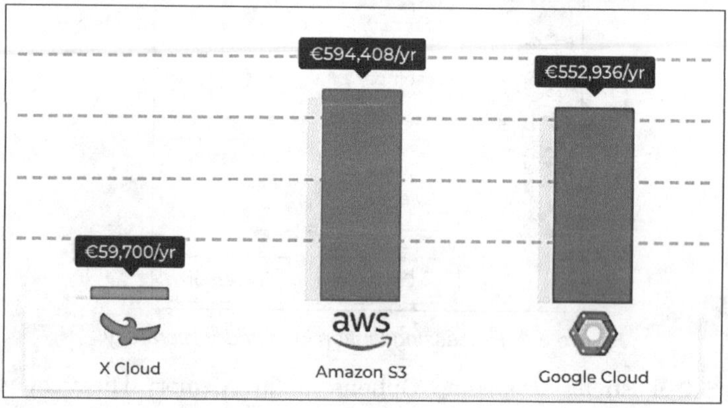

Figure 5.3: *Object Storage by* Amazon S3 and Google Cloud Storage use object storage

Figure 5.3 illustrates a cost comparison of Object Storage services offered by Amazon S3, Google Cloud Storage, and X Cloud (2024).

Object storage is a highly scalable data storage architecture used by cloud providers to store large volumes of unstructured data, such as media files, backups, logs, and archives. Amazon S3 and Google Cloud Storage are among the most popular cloud-based object storage solutions, offering high durability, redundancy, and global accessibility.

The chart indicates that Amazon S3 incurs the highest yearly cost (€594,408/yr), followed closely by Google Cloud Storage (€552,936/yr), while X Cloud offers a significantly lower-cost alternative (€59,700/yr). This comparison suggests that while Amazon S3 and Google Cloud Storage provide enterprise-grade storage with extensive global infrastructure, the cost can be a determining factor for businesses.

5. Cloud-Native and Edge Storage Solutions

- Cloud-based storage integrates with hybrid and multi-cloud environments.
- Edge storage enables real-time data processing closer to the source, reducing latency.

- Edge computing is used in smart cities, IoT networks, and remote surveillance systems.

  Example: Microsoft Azure and AWS Outposts offer edge storage solutions for low-latency computing.

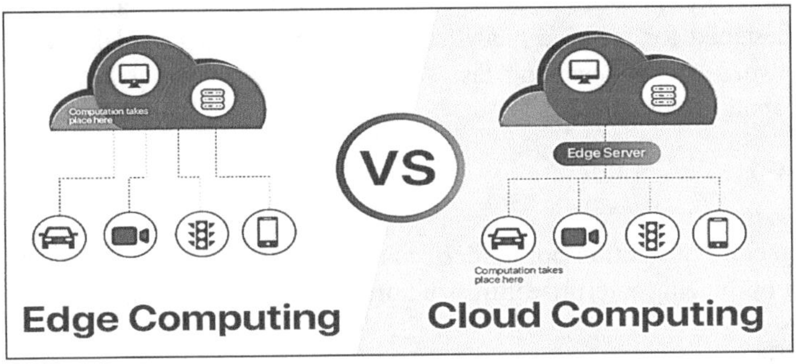

Figure 5.4: Cloud vs. Edge Storage Deployment

Figure 5.4 illustrates the differences between Cloud Computing and Edge Computing in storage deployment, highlighting how data processing is distributed across different architectures.

In Cloud Computing, data processing and storage occur in centralized data centres, where information from various devices is sent to the cloud for computation and analysis. This approach ensures high scalability, extensive computational resources, and centralized management, making it ideal for big data applications, AI training, and large-scale enterprise solutions. However, cloud computing suffers from higher latency and dependency on internet connectivity, which can slow down real-time applications.

In contrast, Edge Computing brings computation closer to the data source, processing information on local edge servers or devices rather than relying solely on remote cloud data centres. This method reduces latency, enhances real-time decision-making, and decreases bandwidth usage, making it particularly beneficial for autonomous vehicles, IoT applications, industrial automation, and smart city infrastructure.

While cloud computing provides vast computational power and centralized security, edge computing enables faster response times and local data processing. Many modern architectures adopt a hybrid approach, where edge computing handles real-time tasks while cloud computing manages long-term data storage and large-scale analysis.

Table 5.1: Comparison of Advanced Storage Technologies

Technology	Speed	Use Case	Key Advantage
NVMe Storage	Ultra-Fast	High-performance computing	Low latency
Storage-Class Memory	Very High	Database acceleration	Persistent memory
AI-Driven Storage	Variable	Cloud optimization	Smart resource allocation
Object Storage	High	Big data analytics	Scalability
Edge Storage	Fast	IoT and remote processing	Reduced network latency

Table 5.1 compares advanced storage technologies, highlighting their speed, primary use cases, and key advantages. NVMe storage delivers ultra-fast performance with low latency, making it ideal for high-performance computing. Storage-Class Memory (SCM) offers very high speeds and persistent memory, enhancing database acceleration. AI-driven storage dynamically optimizes cloud resources, improving efficiency and scalability. Object storage is designed for big data analytics, providing unlimited scalability. Edge storage reduces network latency, enabling fast, localized data processing for IoT and remote computing applications.

Conclusion

Advanced storage technologies are reshaping data management, enabling faster, more scalable, and efficient solutions for modern computing. Understanding these innovations is essential for optimizing enterprise infrastructure, cloud storage, and high-speed computing applications.

The following section will explore Next-Generation Non-Volatile Memory Technologies, detailing innovations in 3D NAND, ReRAM, and MRAM.

5.2 NEXT-GENERATION NON-VOLATILE MEMORY TECHNOLOGIES

Introduction to Non-Volatile Memory (NVM)

Non-volatile memory (NVM) refers to storage devices that retain data even when power is turned off. Traditional storage solutions like HDDs and NAND-based SSDs have limitations in terms of speed, endurance, and scalability. To address these challenges, next-generation NVM technologies have emerged, offering faster access times, higher durability, and improved energy efficiency.

The following advanced NVM technologies are transforming data storage and computing:

1. 3D NAND Flash Memory

- A multi-layered storage technology that stacks multiple layers of NAND cells to increase storage density.
- Provides higher capacity and better endurance than traditional 2D NAND.
- Reduces latency and improves power efficiency in SSDs.

  Example: Samsung V-NAND and Micron 3D NAND SSDs enhance storage performance in enterprise environments.

The following **Figure 5.5** illustrates the 3D NAND Flash Layer Structure, a modern storage technology that enhances memory density and performance compared to traditional 2D NAND.

3D NAND flash memory stacks multiple layers of memory cells vertically, significantly increasing storage capacity without expanding the chip's physical footprint. The diagram highlights alternating layers of Tungsten (W) and Oxide (O), forming a multi-layered architecture that enables higher endurance, better power efficiency, and improved write speeds. The channels allow data to be read and written efficiently, while the word lines (WL) and slits play a critical role in memory addressing and access control.

Unlike 2D NAND, where memory cells are arranged in a single planar layer, 3D NAND overcomes scaling limitations by utilizing vertical stacking, which reduces interference between cells and improves performance and durability. This technology is widely used in solid-state drives (SSDs), mobile devices, and enterprise storage solutions, providing higher speeds, lower latency, and greater reliability in modern computing applications.

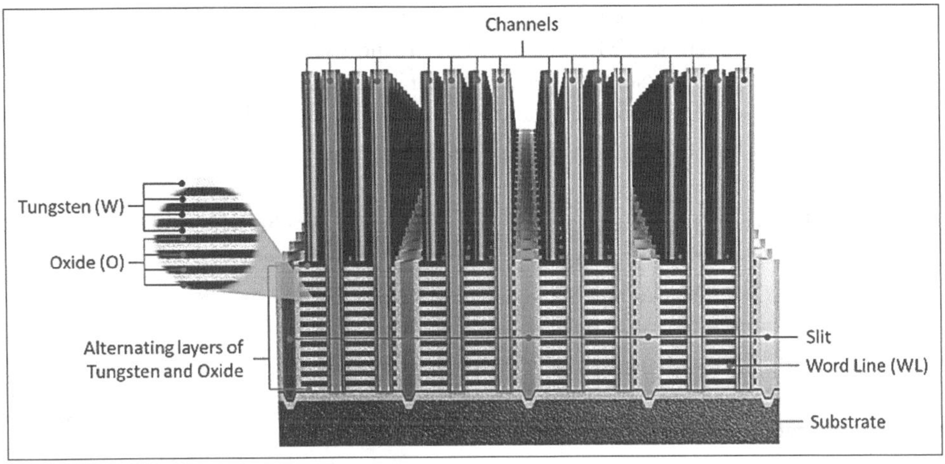

Figure 5.5: *3D NAND Flash Layer Structure*

2. Resistive RAM (ReRAM)

- Uses resistance changes in a metal oxide layer to store data.
- It is faster than traditional NAND and offers higher endurance.
- Used in AI workloads, edge computing, and embedded systems.

  Example: HP Memristor-based ReRAM solutions enhance AI chip performance.

3. Magnetoresistive RAM (MRAM)

- Stores data using magnetic states rather than electrical charges.
- It offers ultra-low latency and consumes less power than DRAM.
- Suitable for real-time processing, IoT devices, and aerospace applications.

  Example: Everspin MRAM technology is used in industrial automation and automotive systems.

Figure 5.6 illustrates the MRAM (Magnetoresistive Random-Access Memory) Data Storage Mechanism within the broader memory hierarchy, highlighting its role in next-generation computing.

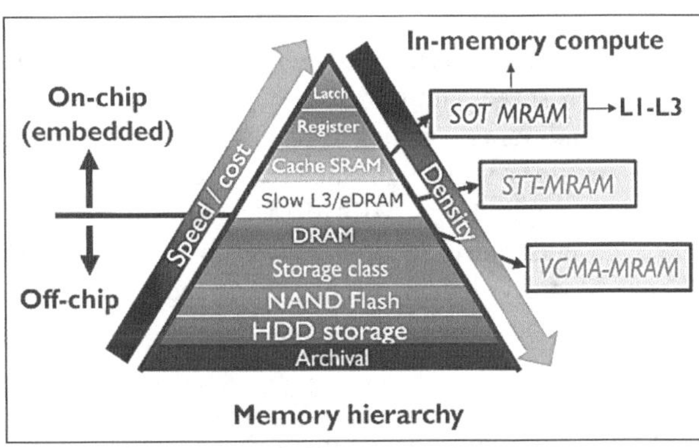

Figure 5.6: *MRAM Data Storage Mechanism*

The memory hierarchy pyramid categorizes storage solutions based on speed, cost, and density. At the top of the hierarchy, on-chip memory like registers, cache SRAM, and slow L3/eDRAM provide high-speed access but at a higher cost and lower density. DRAM and NAND Flash fall in the middle, balancing performance and capacity, while HDD storage and archival memory are at the bottom, offering high-density but slower speeds.

MRAM, particularly SOT-MRAM, STT-MRAM, and VCMA-MRAM, represents an emerging class of in-memory computing technology designed to bridge the gap between high-speed volatile memory (SRAM, DRAM) and non-volatile storage (NAND Flash, HDDs). MRAM operates using magnetic states rather than electrical charges, offering faster read/write speeds, non-volatility, and lower power consumption.

- **SOT-MRAM** (Spin-Orbit Torque MRAM) is targeted for high-speed cache applications (L1-L3).
- **STT-MRAM** (Spin-Transfer Torque MRAM) is an alternative to DRAM with lower power consumption.
- **VCMA-MRAM** (Voltage-Controlled MRAM) focuses on high-density storage with energy-efficient switching mechanisms.

By integrating MRAM into future computing architectures, systems can achieve better performance, increased energy efficiency, and improved endurance, making it a potential successor to traditional DRAM and NAND flash storage.

4. Phase-Change Memory (PCM)

- It uses heat-induced phase transitions in materials to store data.
- Provides speeds closer to DRAM with non-volatility.
- IBM and Intel have developed PCM-based storage-class memory solutions.

  Example: Intel's Optane Memory (based on PCM) bridges the gap between DRAM and SSDs.

Table 5.2: *Comparison of Next-Generation NVM Technologies*

Technology	Speed	Endurance	Use Case
3D NAND	High	Medium	SSDs, Enterprise Storage
ReRAM	Very High	High	AI, Edge Computing
MRAM	Ultra-Fast	Very High	IoT, Industrial Applications
PCM	Moderate	High	Data Centers, AI Systems

Table 5.2 compares next-generation Non-Volatile Memory (NVM) technologies, focusing on speed, endurance, and primary use cases. 3D NAND offers high speed and medium endurance, making it ideal for SSDs and enterprise storage. ReRAM (Resistive RAM) provides very high speed and endurance and is well-suited for AI and edge computing applications. MRAM (Magnetoresistive RAM) delivers ultra-fast speeds with very high endurance, making it ideal for IoT and industrial applications. PCM (Phase-Change Memory) balances moderate speed with high endurance, making it practical for data centres and AI-driven systems.

Conclusion

Next-generation non-volatile memory technologies are revolutionizing storage efficiency, endurance, and speed. These advancements enable faster data access, lower power consumption, and better integration with AI-driven workloads. The following section will cover Energy-Efficient Storage Solutions, exploring how modern storage architectures reduce power consumption and improve sustainability.

5.3 ENERGY-EFFICIENT STORAGE SOLUTIONS

Introduction to Energy-Efficient Storage

With the increasing demand for data storage and computational power, energy efficiency has become a critical factor in designing modern storage solutions. Energy-efficient storage technologies aim to minimize power consumption, reduce heat generation, and extend the lifespan of storage devices, ultimately lowering operational costs and environmental impact.

Several advancements in low-power storage devices, AI-driven energy optimization, and green data centres are transforming the way organizations store and manage data while maintaining energy efficiency.

Key Technologies in Energy-Efficient Storage

1. Low-Power Solid-State Drives (SSDs)

- SSDs consume significantly less power compared to traditional HDDs due to the absence of mechanical parts.
- Modern SSDs feature Dynamic Power Management (DPM) to adjust power consumption based on workload.
- **NVMe SSDs** offer optimized power efficiency with high-speed performance.

  Example: Samsung's PM9A3 NVMe SSD reduces power consumption while maintaining high data transfer speeds in cloud storage environments.

2. AI-Driven Energy Optimization in Storage

- AI algorithms analyze data access patterns to optimize storage tiering.
- Machine learning models predict data retrieval requirements, reducing the energy required for unnecessary read/write operations.
- AI-based cooling management in data centres reduces cooling energy consumption.

  Example: Google's AI-driven data center cooling system reduced energy consumption by 40%.

3. Cold Storage Solutions for Archival Data

- Cold storage is designed for infrequently accessed data using low-power storage devices.
- Technologies like magnetic tapes (LTO), optical discs, and archival HDDs consume minimal energy.
- Cloud providers offer tiered storage solutions, automatically moving archival data to energy-efficient storage.

  Example: AWS Glacier provides a cost-effective, low-energy archival storage solution for long-term data retention.

4. Green Data Centers and Energy-Efficient Storage Infrastructure

- Use of renewable energy sources (solar, win(d) for data centres.
- Implementation of solid-state storage arrays to reduce mechanical energy loss.
- Adoption of liquid cooling systems to lower cooling power consumption.

  Example: Microsoft's Project Natick, an underwater data centre, reduces cooling energy by leveraging deep-sea temperatures.

5. Emerging Technologies in Sustainable Storage

- **DNA Data Storage**: Uses biological molecules to store data at ultra-low power levels.
- **ReRAM (Resistive RAM) and MRAM (Magnetoresistive RAM)**: Offer near-instant access to data while consuming minimal energy.
- **Nanophotonic Storage**: Uses light-based data transfer to reduce electrical power consumption in storage networks.

  Example: University researchers are exploring DNA-based storage, which consumes 100,000 times less energy than conventional hard drives.

Table 5.5 compares energy-efficient storage solutions, highlighting power consumption, use cases, and key benefits. Low-power SSDs provide fast and energy-efficient storage for enterprise and personal use. Cold storage consumes very little power, making it ideal for long-term archival and backup solutions. AI-driven optimization dynamically manages data centre storage, reducing unnecessary power usage. Green data centres focus on sustainable cloud infrastructure, lowering the carbon footprint. DNA storage, a futuristic archival method, offers ultra-low power consumption with high density and minimal energy requirements for long-term data preservation.

Table 5.3: *Comparison of Energy-Efficient Storage Solutions*

Storage Technology	Power Consumption	Use Case	Key Benefit
Low-Power SSDs	Low	Enterprise & Personal Storage	Faster & Energy-Efficient
Cold Storage	Very Low	Archival & Backup	Cost-effective, Long-Term Storage
AI-Driven Optimization	Variable	Data Centers & Cloud	Reduces Unnecessary Power Usage
Green Data Centers	Sustainable	Cloud Infrastructure	Lower Carbon Footprint
DNA Storage	Ultra-Low	Future Archival	High Density, Minimal Energy

Conclusion

Energy-efficient storage solutions play a crucial role in reducing power consumption, operational costs, and environmental impact. With advancements in low-power SSDs, AI-driven storage optimization, green data centres, and emerging sustainable storage technologies, organizations can achieve sustainable and high-performance storage infrastructure.

The following section will explore Storage Security and Data Protection Mechanisms, focusing on best practices for securing stored data against cyber threats and physical failures.

Interesting Facts

- **Power-Saving Prowess:** Low-power SSDs consume dramatically less energy than traditional HDDs, thanks to the absence of mechanical parts.
- **AI for Efficiency:** AI-driven storage optimization can cut energy consumption by predicting data access patterns and adjusting operations in real-time.
- **Cold Storage Economy:** Archival or cold storage solutions, such as AWS Glacier, use minimal energy by keeping rarely accessed data on low-power storage devices.
- **Green Data Centers:** Innovative projects like Microsoft's Project Natick use underwater data centres to leverage natural cooling, dramatically reducing the energy needed for cooling systems.
- **Future of Storage:** Emerging technologies like DNA storage, ReRAM, MRAM, and nanophotonic storage promise ultra-low power consumption while delivering high density and performance.

Video Resources

- **Overview Videos:** Search YouTube for "Energy-Efficient Storage Solutions Explained" or "Low-Power SSD vs. HDD" for animated comparisons of power consumption.
- **Tutorials & Demonstrations:** Look up "AI-Driven Storage Optimization in Data Centers" and "Cold Storage vs. Hot Storage: Energy Impacts" to see real-world applications.
- **Expert Discussions:** Channels like *IEEE Spectrum*, *TechLinked*, and *Linus Tech Tips* provide insights into green data centres and emerging sustainable storage technologies.

Use of ICT

- **Real-Time Monitoring:** ICT systems deploy energy monitoring tools and sensors to track power usage in storage devices, enabling dynamic adjustments to reduce energy waste.
- **Predictive Analytics:** Machine learning models analyze data access patterns to optimize storage tiering and caching, reducing unnecessary read/write operations and energy consumption.
- **Integration with Renewable Energy:** Modern ICT platforms support data centres powered by solar, wind, or other renewable sources, helping to lower the carbon footprint further.

Applications (Real Life/Industrial)

- **Enterprise & Personal Storage:** Low-power SSDs and NVMe solutions are used in laptops, desktops, and servers to boost performance while reducing energy costs.

- **Data Centers & Cloud Services:** AI-driven optimization and green data centre infrastructure help large-scale cloud providers cut energy usage, lower operational costs, and reduce environmental impact.
- **Archival & Backup Systems:** Cold storage solutions, such as magnetic tapes and cloud archival services, provide energy-efficient long-term data retention.
- **Edge & IoT Applications:** Energy-efficient storage at the edge enables real-time data processing in smart cities and IoT networks, minimizing network transmission energy.

Case Study (Environmental/Sustainability/Social/Ethical Issues)

Context

A multinational technology company was facing escalating energy costs and an increased environmental footprint due to outdated, energy-intensive storage systems in its data centres.

Scenario

- **Challenge:** The company's legacy storage, primarily based on HDDs and inefficient SSDs, resulted in high power consumption, excessive heat generation, and frequent cooling demands.
- **Solution:**
  - **Upgrading to Low-Power SSDs:** The company transitioned to NVMe SSDs with Dynamic Power Management (DPM), significantly reducing power draw.
  - **Implementing AI-Driven Optimization:** By deploying AI algorithms to predict data access patterns, the system dynamically adjusts storage tiering and optimizes caching, reducing unnecessary read/write operations.
  - **Adopting Cold Storage:** Archival data was migrated to cold storage solutions like AWS Glacier, which consume minimal power.
  - **Green Data Center Practices:** The data centres integrated renewable energy sources and advanced cooling technologies, such as liquid cooling and innovative designs like underwater data centres.
- **Impact:**
  - **Performance:** Faster data access with lower latency and reduced thermal output.
  - **Sustainability:** A reduction in overall power consumption by up to 40%, lower cooling requirements, and a decreased carbon footprint.
  - **Ethical Leadership:** The initiative enhanced the company's reputation for sustainable practices, demonstrating a strong commitment to environmental stewardship.

Discussion Points

- How can energy-efficient storage reduce operational costs and carbon footprints in large-scale data centres?

- What ethical responsibilities do organizations have in implementing green IT solutions?
- How does AI-driven optimization contribute to both performance gains and sustainability?

Create Inquisitiveness and Curiosity

- **Future Vision:** How might emerging technologies like nanophotonic storage or DNA data storage further minimize energy consumption in future data centres?
- **Design Challenge:** Imagine designing a data centre that runs entirely on renewable energy. What energy-efficient storage solutions and cooling strategies will we choose?
- **Debate Prompt:** Should energy efficiency be prioritized over raw performance in storage systems? What trade-offs are acceptable, and how should they be balanced?
- **Innovation Brainstorm:** Can we propose a hybrid storage model that seamlessly integrates low-power SSDs, AI-driven optimization, and cold storage to achieve both high performance and minimal energy use?

Solved Problems (With Increasing Difficulty Level)

Problem 1 (Basic)

Question

What is the main advantage of low-power SSDs over traditional HDDs in terms of energy consumption?

Solution

Low-power SSDs consume significantly less energy because they have no mechanical parts and utilize dynamic power management to adjust power usage based on workload.

Problem 2 (Intermediate)

Question

Explain how AI-driven energy optimization can reduce power consumption in a data centre.

Solution

AI-driven energy optimization uses machine learning algorithms to analyze data access patterns and predict demand. This enables dynamic adjustments to storage tiering, caching, and cooling systems, thereby reducing unnecessary read/write operations and overall energy consumption.

Problem 3 (Advanced)

Question

Compare cold storage and hot storage in terms of energy consumption and typical use cases.

Solution

- **Cold Storage:** Designed for infrequently accessed data, cold storage solutions like magnetic tapes or cloud archival services consume very little power, making them ideal for long-term data retention and backups.
- **Hot Storage:** Used for frequently accessed data, hot storage systems (such as SSDs or active HDDs) have higher energy consumption due to continuous read/write operations. They are optimized for speed and immediate access but at a higher power cost.

Cold storage is more energy-efficient for archival purposes, while hot storage prioritizes performance over energy savings.

Problem 4 (Challenging)

Question

A cloud service provider wants to reduce its data centre's energy consumption while maintaining high performance. Propose a comprehensive storage strategy that integrates *low-power SSDs*, *AI-driven optimization*, cold storage, and green data centre practices. Justify your approach and discuss potential trade-offs.

Solution

Proposed Strategy

- **Low-Power SSDs:** Replace traditional HDDs with NVMe SSDs featuring Dynamic Power Management to lower energy consumption.
- **AI-Driven Optimization:** Implement AI algorithms to monitor data access patterns and dynamically adjust storage tiering and caching, thereby reducing unnecessary disk activity.
- **Cold Storage:** Use cold storage solutions (e.g., AWS Glacier) for archival data to minimize power usage for data that is infrequently accessed.
- **Green Data Center Practices:** Integrate renewable energy sources (solar, win(d) and advanced cooling techniques (liquid cooling, underwater data centres) to lower the carbon footprint further.

Justification

- **Performance:** NVMe SSDs and AI-driven optimization ensure rapid data access and reduced latency.
- **Scalability:** Cold storage allows for cost-effective, long-term data retention without excessive energy use.
- **Sustainability:** Green data centre practices and renewable energy integration help reduce overall energy consumption and environmental impact.

Trade-Offs

- **Cost:** The initial investment for high-performance, low-power storage and renewable energy infrastructure may be high.
- **Complexity:** Integrating multiple advanced technologies increases system complexity and requires robust management systems.

- **Data Access:** Data in cold storage may have longer retrieval times, which is acceptable for archival purposes but not for real-time applications.

5.4 STORAGE SECURITY AND DATA PROTECTION MECHANISMS

Introduction to Storage Security

With the increasing volume of digital data, securing stored information has become a top priority for businesses, governments, and individuals. Storage security mechanisms protect data from unauthorized access, corruption, loss, and cyber threats. These mechanisms ensure data confidentiality, integrity, and availability, adhering to industry standards and regulatory requirements.

Storage security covers various techniques, including encryption, access control, redundancy, and backup strategies, to mitigate risks associated with cyberattacks, data breaches, and hardware failures.

Key Storage Security Mechanisms

1. Data Encryption for Secure Storage

- Encrypting data at rest, in transit, and use prevents unauthorized access.
- **Hardware-based encryption (Self-Encrypting Drives - SEDs)** provides built-in encryption with minimal performance impact.
- **Software-based encryption (BitLocker, VeraCrypt, AES-256)** secures data at the file or disk level.

  Example: BitLocker encryption in Windows secures system drives against unauthorized access.

2. Role-Based Access Control (RBA(c) and Authentication

- Implements user roles and permissions to restrict access based on authority levels.
- Uses Multi-Factor Authentication (MF(a) to enhance identity verification.
- Enforces least privilege access policies to minimize security risks.

  Example: **Amazon** S3's IAM (Identity and Access Management) policies restrict data access to authorized personnel only.

3. Redundancy and Data Replication for Fault Tolerance

- **RAID (Redundant Array of Independent Disks)** configurations improve **data redundancy and reliability**.
- **Cloud-based replication** ensures copies of data are available in multiple locations.
- **Snapshot-based backups** allow recovery of previous file versions in case of corruption.

  Example: RAID 6 and RAID 10 configurations provide high fault tolerance for enterprise storage systems.

4. Secure Backup Strategies and Disaster Recovery

- The 3-2-1 backup rule (3 copies of data, 2 different storage media, 1 offsite backup) prevents data loss.

- Automated incremental and differential backups optimize storage usage and backup efficiency.
- Disaster recovery solutions such as geo-redundant storage (GRS) ensure business continuity after failures.

  Example: Microsoft Azure Backup automates secure data backups with geo-redundancy.

5. Protection Against Ransomware and Cyber Threats

- **Immutable storage** prevents ransomware from modifying or deleting critical data.
- **AI-driven anomaly detection** identifies suspicious file access patterns and prevents unauthorized encryption.
- **Zero-trust architecture** ensures that no device or user is trusted by default.

  Example: AWS S3 Object Lock enforces immutability, making data tamper-proof against cyberattacks.

Table 5.4 Compares various storage security mechanism, outlining their purpose and key benefits. Encryption safeguards data by preventing unauthorized access and ensuring confidentally. Role-based Access Control (RBA(c) and Mult-Factor Authenction (MF(a) restrict access based on user roles, enhancing security against unauthorized access. RAID and replication provide redundancy, minimizing data loss risks. Backup strategies ensure data protection against failures, enabling effecient disaster recovery. Immutable storage protects against ransomware attacks, maintaining data integrity by preventing unauthorized modifications.

Table 5.4: *Comparison of Storage Security Mechanisms*

Security Mechanism	Purpose	Key Benefit
Encryption	Protects data from unauthorized access	Ensures confidentiality
RBAC & MFA	Restricts access based on roles	Prevents unauthorized access
RAID & Replication	Ensures redundancy	Prevents data loss
Backup Strategies	Secures data against failures	Enables disaster recovery
Immutable Storage	Prevents ransomware attacks	Ensures data integrity

Conclusion

Storage security mechanisms are essential to protect data from unauthorized access, cyber threats, and hardware failures. Organizations implement encryption, access control, redundancy, and backup strategies to ensure data confidentiality, availability, and integrity.

The following section will focus on Future Trends in Storage Technologies, exploring innovations in quantum storage, DNA-based storage, and AI-driven data management.

5.5 FUTURE TRENDS IN STORAGE TECHNOLOGIES

Introduction to Emerging Storage Technologies

As technology advances, the demand for faster, more efficient, and higher-capacity storage solutions continues to grow. Innovations in quantum storage, DNA-based storage, and AI-driven data management are shaping the future of data storage, promising unparalleled performance, scalability, and sustainability.

These future trends aim to address current limitations in data density, retrieval speed, security, and energy consumption, making storage more adaptive to the evolving digital landscape.

Key Innovations in Future Storage Technologies

1. Quantum Storage

- It uses principles of quantum mechanics to store and retrieve data at ultra-high speeds.
- Employs qubits and quantum entanglement for exponentially larger storage capacities.
- Provides near-instantaneous data processing, eliminating traditional bottlenecks.

  For example, IBM and Google are developing quantum memory models for ultra-fast computing applications.

2. DNA-Based Data Storage

- Encodes digital data into synthetic DNA strands, enabling ultra-dense storage.
- Offers thousands of years of durability with minimal energy consumption.
- Potentially replaces traditional storage devices with biological storage media.

  Example: Microsoft and the University of Washington successfully demonstrated DNA-based archival storage.

3. AI-Driven Intelligent Storage Management

- AI optimizes data storage, retrieval, and tiering using predictive analytics.
- Reduces latency and redundancy by automatically classifying frequently used data.
- Enhances security through AI-based anomaly detection and automated threat prevention.

  Example: Google Cloud and AWS use AI-driven storage tiering to optimize cloud performance.

4. Holographic Storage

- Stores data in three-dimensional light patterns, vastly increasing storage density.
- Enables multi-layered data writing, reducing read/write time significantly.
- Suitable for high-performance computing, media archiving, and enterprise applications.

  Example: IBM and Hitachi are investing in holographic storage solutions for large-scale data centres.

5. Neuromorphic Storage Systems

- Mimics the human brain's neural networks to optimize memory usage.

- It uses non-volatile memory with AI-driven processing to improve efficiency.
- It is ideal for edge computing, IoT, and real-time analytics.

  Example: Intel's neuromorphic computing research integrates storage and processing in AI systems.

Table 5.5: *Comparison of Future Storage Technologies*

Technology	Storage Density	Speed	Energy Efficiency	Use Case
Quantum Storage	Extremely High	Ultra-Fast	High	High-Performance Computing, AI Workloads
DNA Storage	Ultra-High	Slow	Very High	Archival, Biological Data Storage
AI-Driven Storage	Variable	Adaptive	Medium	Cloud, Edge Computing
Holographic Storage	High	High	Low	Enterprise Data Centers
Neuromorphic Storage	Moderate	Fast	High	AI, IoT, Edge Analytics

Table 5.5 compares future storage technologies, focusing on storage density, speed, energy efficiency, and primary use cases. Quantum storage offers exceptionally high density and ultra-fast speeds, making it ideal for high-performance computing and AI workloads. DNA storage provides ultra-high density and exceptional energy efficiency, which is best suited for long-term archival and biological data storage. AI-driven storage dynamically adapts to workloads, optimizing cloud and edge computing environments. Holographic storage offers high-speed data retrieval for enterprise data centres. In contrast, neuromorphic storage is designed for AI, IoT, and edge analytics, balancing moderate density, fast speeds, and high energy efficiency.

Conclusion

Future storage technologies are set to redefine the way data is stored, accessed, and managed, offering solutions that are faster, more scalable, and energy-efficient. From quantum storage and DNA-based encoding to AI-driven intelligent storage and neuromorphic memory, these advancements will shape the next generation of digital infrastructure.

With ongoing research and development, these cutting-edge technologies are expected to become commercially viable in the coming years, revolutionizing enterprise storage, cloud computing, and high-performance applications.

SUMMARY

This unit explored cutting-edge storage technologies that are transforming the way data is stored, accessed, and managed. Key topics covered include:

- Next-Generation Storage Technologies: Innovations such as NVMe storage, Storage-Class Memory (SCM), and AI-driven storage optimization.
- Energy-Efficient Storage Solutions: The role of low-power SSDs, AI-driven power management, and green data centres in reducing energy consumption.
- Storage Security and Data Protection: Implementation of encryption, access control, redundancy mechanisms, and ransomware protection.

- Future Storage Trends: Emerging technologies like quantum storage, DNA-based storage, holographic memory, and neuromorphic storage.

These advancements ensure that future storage infrastructures are highly scalable, efficient, and secure, capable of meeting the increasing demand for high-speed and large-scale data processing.

Interesting Facts

- **Quantum Leap:** Quantum storage uses qubits and quantum entanglement to potentially store exponentially more data than classical storage, promising near-instant data retrieval.
- **Biological Breakthrough:** DNA-based storage can theoretically store petabytes of data in a single gram, offering millennia-long durability with minimal energy consumption.
- **AI at the Helm:** AI-driven intelligent storage management systems are revolutionizing data centres by predicting data access patterns, optimizing tiering, and even enhancing security.
- **Three-Dimensional Innovation:** *Holographic storage leverages 3D* light patterns to write and read data in multiple layers, significantly increasing storage density.
- **Brain-Inspired Memory:** Neuromorphic storage systems mimic neural networks, integrating processing with storage to support rapid, energy-efficient computing at the edge.

Video Resources

- **Overview Videos:** Search YouTube for "Future Storage Technologies" or "Quantum Storage Explained" for animated explanations and expert insights.
- **Tutorials & Demos:** Look for "DNA Data Storage: How It Works" and "AI-Driven Storage Optimization in Cloud Environments" to see practical demonstrations.
- **Expert Panels:** Channels such as *IEEE Spectrum*, *Linus Tech Tips*, and *TechLinked* provide in-depth discussions on emerging trends like holographic and neuromorphic storage.

Use of ICT

- **Simulation & Modeling:** Advanced ICT tools enable engineers to simulate quantum and holographic storage architectures, predicting performance before physical prototypes are built.
- **Cloud Integration:** ICT platforms are essential for integrating AI-driven storage management into cloud infrastructures, dynamically optimizing data placement and retrieval.
- **Real-Time Analytics:** Machine learning and real-time monitoring systems ensure that emerging storage technologies are deployed efficiently and securely in large-scale environments.

Applications (Real Life/Industrial)

- **High-Performance Computing (HP(c):** Quantum storage and neuromorphic storage promise ultra-fast data access for complex AI workloads and scientific simulations.

- **Archival Systems:** DNA-based storage offers unparalleled density and longevity, making it ideal for long-term data preservation in national archives and research institutions.
- **Cloud & Edge Computing:** AI-driven storage and object storage systems support scalable, low-latency applications for cloud providers and smart city IoT networks.
- **Enterprise Data Centers:** Holographic storage is being explored for high-speed, high-density data centres that require rapid read/write operations for media and large-scale analytics.

Case Study (Environmental/Sustainability/Social/Ethical Issues)

Context

A multinational research institution needed to overhaul its archival storage solutions to handle exponential data growth while reducing its environmental impact.

Scenario

- **Challenge:** Traditional storage systems were reaching their limits in capacity, energy efficiency, and longevity, leading to excessive power consumption and increased e-waste.
- **Solution**
    - **DNA-Based Storage Pilot:** The institution initiated a pilot project using DNA data storage to archive historical research data. This method promised ultra-high density and minimal energy usage.
    - **Quantum Storage Research:** Simultaneously, the research team collaborated with industry partners (like IBM and Google) to develop experimental quantum storage models for real-time data processing.
    - **AI-Driven Management:** The institution integrated AI-driven storage optimization to automatically tier and manage data between high-speed quantum storage for active data and DNA storage for archival purposes.
- **Impact:**
    - **Environmental Benefit:** Reduced energy consumption and a significantly lower carbon footprint due to the ultra-low power requirements of DNA storage.
    - **Operational Efficiency:** Faster retrieval times for active data and highly secure long-term archival, enhancing research capabilities.
    - **Ethical Leadership:** The project positioned the institution as a leader in sustainable and innovative data storage, balancing cutting-edge technology with environmental responsibility.

Discussion Points

- How do emerging storage technologies like DNA and quantum storage contribute to reducing environmental impact?
- What ethical considerations should organizations address when adopting experimental storage methods for critical data?

- In what ways can AI-driven optimization further enhance the sustainability and efficiency of future storage infrastructures?

Create Inquisitiveness and Curiosity

- **Future Vision:** How might quantum storage, when fully realized, transform the landscape of big data and artificial intelligence?
- **Design Challenge:** Imagine we are tasked with designing a global archival system that lasts thousands of years with minimal energy input. Which future storage technologies will we integrate, and how will we ensure data integrity over such long periods?
- **Debate Prompt:** Should organizations invest in experimental storage technologies like neuromorphic or holographic storage despite the high initial costs and uncertainties, or stick with proven methods until the new technologies mature?
- **Innovation Brainstorm:** Can we conceptualize a hybrid storage system that combines the ultra-high density of DNA storage with the speed of quantum storage? What potential challenges would need to be overcome for seamless integration?

Solved Problems (With Increasing Difficulty Level)

Problem 1 (Basic)

Question

What is one primary advantage of using quantum storage over traditional storage systems?

Solution

Quantum storage leverages quantum mechanics to store and retrieve data at ultra-high speeds with potentially much larger capacities than traditional binary storage, drastically reducing data retrieval times.

Problem 2 (Intermediate)

Question

Explain how DNA-based data storage achieves ultra-high storage density and what makes it energy-efficient.

Solution

DNA-based storage encodes digital data into synthetic DNA strands, which can store vast amounts of information in a minuscule physical space (e.g., 1 gram of DNA can hold up to 215 petabytes). Additionally, DNA does not require continuous power to retain data, making it highly energy-efficient compared to electronic storage.

Problem 3 (Advanced)

Question

Describe how AI-driven intelligent storage management optimizes data placement and reduces latency in a cloud environment.

Solution

AI-driven storage management uses machine learning algorithms to analyze data access patterns and predict future usage. By dynamically adjusting caching policies, storage tiering, and data placement, AI ensures that frequently accessed data is stored on high-speed media (such as NVMe or quantum storage). In contrast, infrequently accessed data is moved to more cost-effective, lower-energy storage solutions. This reduces overall latency and enhances system performance while optimizing energy consumption.

Problem 4 (Challenging)

Question

A multinational corporation is planning to build a next-generation data centre that incorporates future storage technologies to support AI and big data analytics while being environmentally sustainable. Propose a comprehensive storage strategy that integrates quantum storage, DNA-based storage, AI-driven management, and holographic storage. Justify our proposal and discuss potential trade-offs.

Solution

Proposed Strategy

- **Primary High-Speed Tier**
    - **Quantum Storage:** Deploy experimental quantum storage systems to handle real-time data processing and ultra-fast analytics for AI workloads.
- **Archival Tier**
    - **DNA-Based Storage:** Utilize DNA-based storage for long-term archival of research and historical data, leveraging its ultra-high density and energy efficiency.
- **Optimization & Management**
    - **AI-Driven Intelligent Storage:** Integrate AI algorithms to manage data across tiers, dynamically adjusting storage tiering, caching, and data replication to optimize performance and energy usage.
- **Supplementary Tier**
    - **Holographic Storage:** Use holographic storage in areas requiring high-density, multi-layered data storage, such as media archives or large-scale enterprise data centres.

Justification

- **Performance:** Quantum storage provides unparalleled speed, which is essential for AI and real-time analytics.
- **Scalability & Efficiency:** DNA-based storage offers long-term, low-energy archival capabilities, while holographic storage delivers high-density storage for massive datasets.
- **Optimization:** AI-driven management ensures seamless data placement across tiers, balancing performance with cost and energy efficiency.

Trade-Offs

- **Cost:** Advanced technologies like quantum and DNA storage currently have high initial costs and may require significant investment in R&D.
- **Complexity:** Integrating multiple emerging storage technologies increases system complexity and may demand advanced management tools and specialized expertise.
- **Maturity:** Some technologies (e.g., quantum storage) are still experimental, which may lead to risks in scalability and reliability in a production environment.

This hybrid strategy aims to maximize performance and scalability while reducing energy consumption and ensuring long-term data integrity, though it must be balanced against higher costs and integration challenges.

EXERCISES

1. Subjective Questions (Conceptual and Analytical)

1. Compare and contrast NVMe storage and traditional SATA-based storage solutions.
2. How does AI-driven storage management improve efficiency and optimize data retrieval?
3. Explain the role of RAID configurations in ensuring storage redundancy and fault tolerance.
4. Discuss the advantages of DNA-based storage over traditional storage devices.
5. Describe how quantum storage differs from current non-volatile memory technologies.
6. What are the key security risks in cloud-based storage, and how can they be mitigated?
7. Explain the 3-2-1 backup strategy and why it is considered best practice for data protection.
8. How does neuromorphic storage emulate the functionality of the human brain in data processing?
9. Compare holographic storage and SSD storage in terms of efficiency and application.
10. Discuss the environmental benefits of adopting green data centres and sustainable storage technologies.

2. Objective Questions (Multiple-Choice and True/False)

Multiple-Choice Questions (MCQs)

1. Which storage technology is based on quantum entanglement for ultra-fast data retrieval?
   (a) NVMe (b) Holographic Storage
   (c) Quantum Storage (d) DNA Storage
2. Which of the following is not an advantage of using SSDs over HDDs?
   (a) Higher speed (b) Lower power consumption
   (c) Higher mechanical durability (d) Greater storage density

3. AI-driven storage management primarily helps in:
   (a) Increasing energy consumption
   (b) Optimizing data placement and tiering
   (c) Slowing down retrieval processes
   (d) Eliminating hardware redundancy
4. What is the key principle behind DNA-based storage?
   (a) Using synthetic DNA strands to encode data
   (b) Storing data in traditional magnetic disks
   (c) Using neural networks to optimize retrieval
   (d) Compressing data into nanostructures
5. Which of the following is a major challenge of holographic storage?
   (a) Limited scalability (b) Slow retrieval speeds
   (c) High cost and complexity (d) Limited application in enterprises

True/False Questions

1. Quantum storage can store and process data using superposition and entanglement. *(True/False)*
2. Cloud storage automatically encrypts all stored data, making additional security measures unnecessary. *(True/False)*
3. DNA storage can store massive amounts of data in an extremely small physical space. *(True/False)*
4. AI-driven storage solutions can detect anomalies and cyber threats in real time. *(True/False)*
5. Holographic storage is based on two-dimensional data writing techniques. *(True/False)*

TEACHER'S KNOW MORE

For educators and advanced learners, additional resources and insights include:

- **AI and Predictive Storage Management:** The future of AI-driven data retrieval and workload optimization.
- **Quantum Computing and Storage:** The role of quantum memory in shaping next-generation data centres.
- **Regulatory Compliance in Secure Storage:** Understanding standards like GDPR, HIPAA, and PCI DSS for enterprise data security.
- **Hands-on Labs for Emerging Storage Technologies:** Practical exercises on NVMe installation, RAID configuration, and AI-based storage monitoring.
- **Trends in Green Storage Solutions:** Research on carbon-neutral data centres, energy-efficient memory, and sustainable storage.